Arise

My Message Is In My Mess

DEDICATION

To my father, Deacon Willard Jones.

When I started writing for and compiling the stories in this book, you were still with us. As I write this, it has been a month since your final rest. Every now and again I can't help but get choked up – and not just because of the fact that you are no longer physically here. In life, your business savvy inspired me to do things on my own, to dream big as my church says. Any time I had an idea or a project, you encouraged me every step of the way. "You can do it, Nisi!" and "Keep going, Nisi!" It was a simple gesture, but it meant the world to me. I long for it even more now that I can no longer hear your voice. As I move on to the next phase of publishing this book, putting it out there to make my Godly-inspired mark on the world, I know that you are up there watching me. "Go, Nisi!"
I hear you loud and clear.

To my sisters, Sheila and Anita:

Words cannot express how deep my love for you continues to flow. Not a day goes by that I don't think of the both of you. I dedicate this book, and all my work, to your legacy. You shall not be forgotten. Without the memory of your encouragement and belief in me, I would not be where I am today.

To my brother-in-law, Charlie:

You were always my number one supporter. No matter what curve balls life threw at you, you never let me down – you *always* showed up. I could not publish this book without dedicating it to you as well.

Table of Contents

ABOUT THE BOOK

This book, like God's love, is for all people. However, I would like to be as clear and transparent as possible: this is a Christian-based, Bible-based book. I have, and will continue to, put my faith in my Lord and Savior Jesus Christ.

I believe that through my testimony, and the testimony of the authors, the lives of people from all faiths and walks of life can be transformed; that people of every hue, creed, nationality, and background can be set free.

ACKNOWLEDGMENTS

"My broken pieces have become and are becoming God's masterpiece."
—Dr. Kiana Battle

First, giving honor to God, my Lord and Savior Jesus Christ, from whom all blessings flow. I can't thank Him enough for bringing me to this point in my life. It has taken a while for me to get here, but better late than never! I would like to thank God for giving me this vision and putting the right people in my life when I needed them. I thank God for each and every person attached to this project: for the effort they put in, sometimes for little to no pay, simply because they believed in the vision that He gave to me and the purpose and plan that He has for my life.

To my mother and father, Cassie and Willard Jones: it has taken me as many years as I've been alive to truly understand how much of a blessing it has been to be your child. I could not have asked for better parents. Through all the years of the messes I've been through, often of my own doing, you both have been there for me. I have witnessed you giving to others time and time again, without receiving anything in return; I get my generous spirit from your example. I love you both so much and am so glad that you have been able to witness my transformation, growth, and success.

To my Aunt Elaine Exum: you are my mother's older sister, but you have been like a second mother to me my entire life. I thank God for the role you have had in my life. Along with my mother, you were the matriarch of this family. As a youngster I knew I could go to you even when I couldn't go to my own mother. You were (and still are) my encourager and your righteous prayers for me continue to availeth much. I just want to say thank you for being a solid rock I could rest on, and a sympathetic listening ear.

To my Aunt Carolyn Altman: We don't see each other or talk much, but since I was a young girl you always made me feel special and good about myself in a world that sometimes tried to break me down. I hold you in my heart and the way your eyes light up when you talk about my endeavors lets me know that you hold me in yours, too. I will never forget the positivity you continue to bring to my life.

To Latoya Smith, my editor: You are like family to me. I feel so blessed to be working with you. You have offered me your expertise and gone above and beyond the call to bring this book to life. Thank you for your careful attention to detail, your standard of excellence in writing, and your passion and caring for this project.

To Carol Sankar: You have played such an important role in this project and in my growth as an entrepreneur. You were the one who told me that my story is a ministry in itself; you helped me to see my worth. Through your company, CSE Inc., I have been able to expand my vision for myself and Azz1 Productions. Without your insight, encouragement, and expertise, I don't know where I would be.

To my cousin, Denarii Monroe, my administrator: I've never been too good with computers or technology, but I believe that God put you in my life to fill that gap. I can thank so many people, but without your assistance and belief in me, this project would not make it to its completion. You helped me organize the book itself, say the things I didn't know how to say, and brainstorm ideas for how to put this thing together. You gave of your time and talents for little pay and, although we're family, I know that you didn't have to do it, but you did. I can't thank you enough because words cannot express how important your contributions have been. Thank you so much!

To Christopher Buckley: I have worked with you before, and I believe that your work speaks for itself. As the designer of this book's front and back cover and inside, you have been such a blessing in my life and I appreciate you. Whenever I needed assistance, you've never told me no. No matter what other obligations you'd committed to in your life, you never forgot me and always came through. Thank you.

To Minister Michael Robinson: My Photographer, thank you for taking the time to make the other women authors and me LOOK and FEEL like the beautiful Queens that we are. We had an amazing photo shoot that was more like spending time with family. God's love and blessings were in the air and it shows in the outcome of your work! May He continue to bless you and your ministries, both inside and outside of the walls of the church!

To my church home, The Cathedral at Miracle: The importance of your presence in my life is immeasurable. In the sanctuary I can be free in the spirit and lay all of my issues before the Lord. I am welcome there. My vision for this book would not have existed without your ministry in my life. I cannot thank you all enough for your words of encouragement through the word and spirit of God, for encouraging me in my walk with Christ, and helping me to grow. It is through that growth that this book was birthed. To Bishop David B. Gates, the spiritual father of this house: thank you for heeding God's call for His purpose in your life. It has been through your purpose and ministry that I was able to find my own. I thank God for giving you a ministry that excels in deliverance; without mine, I would not be where I am today.

And last but certainly not least, to the contributing authors of this book: Kelly, Sonia, Zavier, Bevelyn, Kavon, Monique, Desiree, Felisia, Otis, Kareem, Jonea, and Tonya. It takes a very special person to be vulnerable enough to tell their story. Once it's on the page it becomes real and I know that's not easy. To have stuck with it speaks volumes to me; that you believe in me as a woman of God, in the purpose of this book, and its ability to heal, deliver, and set free. Through our many one-on-ones together, I feel like I have created a special bond with you all. I cannot wait to take this project to the next level. Oh the places we will go!

CHAPTER ONE

Nisi's Prayer

Father, in the name of the only One who has secured our victory on Calvary, borne our sins and carried our sorrows; the One who was pierced and bruised so we can walk in liberty—Jesus Christ the risen One—we give thanks. We thank You because our pain can be healed, our shame eradicated, and our past woven beautifully into the fabric of our present and future. With our guilt erased, we can walk in the glorious light of Your love.

Thank You, Father, for these selfless courageous writers willing to momentarily lift the veil that covers their lives to share with us wounds healed by Your touch. Father, let Your uncontainable blessing saturate the lives of each author who has contributed to this volume. Let this be the beginning of an explosion of gifts and talents in the world of literature, proclaiming Your love for us and Your desire to heal all of our hurting places. Restore to them a thousand fold all they have poured out to so many.

Show us how to find the point of thankfulness in ALL things, and teach us how to love. Teach us how to love You, ourselves, and each other. Reader—yes, you— we invite you to read with an open heart and be prepared for a phenomenal blessing as you lay your burdens down for the joy, peace, healing, and liberty of our Lord. I ask these blessings in the name that is above every name: Jesus the Christ, the risen One.

Amen.

Purpose in My Pain

"And let us not be weary in well doing: for in due season we shall reap, if we faint not."
Galatians 6:9

My passion is to be a voice for change and empowerment for the suffering. Today I live a life that is full of joy and a heart filled with forgiveness, but that was not always the case.

My name is Denise Newsome. I grew up in Roosevelt, Long Island in New York. I had a mother, a father, and three sisters. We lived in a nice house with a big backyard and a swing set.

On the surface, most people would say I had the perfect childhood. And though it's true that many people have had it worse than me, my life has not been a bed of roses.

I've been used and abused. I've used and abused others. I've been incarcerated. I grew up plagued with troubles in a dysfunctional and abusive household. I was always in fear, pushing my feelings deep down within so I wouldn't be a bother to anyone, including myself.

It worked as a child, but as an adult, it became a problem for me. I realize now that the door to my heart was locked shut, and I didn't have the key. I wasn't given the opportunity to learn about emotions.

I didn't think that I could go to my parents; they had their own problems. My father took care of the bills and made sure we had what we needed. My mother took care of the home; her hands were full.

My father was controlling and violent in those days. One of my sisters turned to the streets and drugs, another turned to partying. I just acted out in any way possible.

Because I couldn't identify, express, or manage my own feelings, it made understanding others' feelings difficult, which made making sense of relationships hard. I didn't understand why I did certain things; relationships were just so confusing to me.

With all these issues, I didn't think my feelings mattered; other people came first. It was difficult to say "no" when people asked me for things and almost impossible to ask for help. I had a lot of compassion for others but very little for myself. I believed in my heart that I was here to service other people, but I wasn't allowed or worthy enough to have my own feelings and needs.

It was second nature to me to wear the mask of a happy person. I was always the loudest in a group and made a habit of finding something to joke about and laugh at, even at the expense of others.

I began experimenting and started experiencing depression as well. I felt lifeless, isolated, empty, and angry. I was so full of negative thoughts that I would go so far as to ask myself, "Why live?"

All of this combined made me an exceptional abuser in relationships of all kinds. At one point, I even considered myself a bully.

Despite growing up in the church with a mother who preached and lived by the Gospel, the pain of a troubled past haunted me continuously.

Because of the experiences I had and saw others have with men, I found myself attracted to the same sex at an early age. Being incarcerated allowed me to come out with it. I wanted the world to know, I had to let it show. I started out as a femme, but I didn't feel pretty. As time went on, my look and image changed; I became more of an aggressive woman, wearing men's clothing. I felt handsome.

I was always the dominant one in my relationships with women. Having that mindset, I became controlling and abusive in every way possible. I loved that life; I felt at home and identified as a lesbian for eighteen years.

In 1998, while incarcerated, I lost my sister to an untimely death at the age of twenty-nine. It was hard for me. We were very close, but my incarceration meant that I had to mourn alone. I didn't have my family to comfort me nor was I able to comfort them.

Eventually, being behind the four dim walls of prison, I had plenty of time to look over my life. I realized I had some serious issues. I was mentally, emotionally, verbally, physically, and sexually abused by both men and women. In turn, I became abusive.

I was a pure mess and realized just how dysfunctional I really was. I wanted help. I wanted to live a normal life, so I took every program that was offered to help rehabilitate Nisi. It was very painful to see myself for who I really was and had been. My life is a testament to the saying, "Hurt people hurt people," including oneself.

After years of feeling lost, I returned to my roots and sought refuge in the church. Silently in the background, I realized I wanted more out of life. I watched as death and despair tore my family apart and decided it was time to make peace with my past.

It was at that moment that the layers of pain began to fall away. Hurt, guilt, shame, and more began to unravel and I started to let the trouble and bitterness of my past fade away.

In 2012, at the age of forty-eight, my life shifted. Stepping into Miracle Christian Center, under the leadership of Bishop David B. Gates, was life-changing for me.

Today, I am firmly committed to my new happy and I'm hopeful that God will bless me with love once again. My first journey into writing was the creation of the novel Misty's Blood. I used the pen name Sincerly Yours. I decided to go with a fake name because I was ashamed of my name. I didn't like myself, so I couldn't like my name! I was embarrassed by my story and wanted to hide behind the wall of a pseudonym.

In my growth and renewal, I have come to believe in the power of storytelling. Everyone on this earth has a story to tell. Some are sad, some are uplifting, some are powerful, and every story is unique. But everyone has something in their heart that needs to be shared. This is what all my work is meant to do—tell our stories, and I am on a mission.

However, I write not to entertain, but to influence hearts toward positive change. You can benefit from my lessons, sparing you from learning life the hard way. And if you've already been down similar roads, you can benefit from knowing that you, too, can make it out to the other side.

My journey is meant to make a difference. My hope and prayer is that with every page that you turn, with every moment of pain and triumph that is written within this book, you will be reminded that you are who God says you are.

From stories about suicide and instability to cancer and a crisis of faith, you can't help but be touched by the vulnerability and strength that God has bestowed upon His people.

As you continue on to the next chapters, allow God to speak to you through our words and experiences. What is it that you need to be healed, delivered, and set free from? Which parts of your past do you still hold on to that needs letting go? Where can you get the strength and courage to map out, plan, and follow your dreams, your purpose?

Don't let your mess stop you from prospering! Don't be selfish; stories are meant to be shared.

We can stop generational cycles from repeating themselves; we can begin collective healing, but the only way the world can change is if we open up our mouths and tell our stories.

YOUR MESSAGE IS IN YOUR MESS. ARISE!
TO BE CONTINUED!

Questions for Reflection

1.   A vision board is "a tool used to help clarify, concentrate, and maintain focus on a specific life goal." It is a collage of images, pictures, and affirmations of your dreams that you can hang near you to remind you of your purpose. What has God put in your heart to do? What is your passion? List three things below that you would like to achieve in life (publish a book, travel to another country, start a business, finish college, buy a house or car, etc.) Use this exercise to fuel your determination and create your own vision board.

_____

_____

_____

_____

_____

_____

2.   Think about and write down obstacles that may be preventing you from achieving your goals, whether they are caused by yourself or forces outside of your control. Use this space to replace those obstacles with scriptures that affirm your purpose and God's hand in your life. Meditate on them daily.

_____

_____

_____

_____

_____

_____

CHAPTER TWO

Kelly's Prayer

Father God, in the name of Jesus, I come boldly before the throne of grace, thanking You for being God! I thank You for every season of my life, good and bad. I thank You for Your constant protection. I thank You for Your grace and mercy that You have bestowed upon me, allowing me to remain here to tell my story. Father, I pray that You touch and open the hearts of my readers. I ask that they may receive healing and peace in their lives as they read how You've healed me from cancer, depression, and the thought of suicide. God, I ask that Your will be done in every readers' life.

I plead the blood of Jesus over every spirit of sickness, depression, suicide, unforgiveness, hatred, low self-esteem and every ungodly spirit that has attached itself or is trying to attach itself to those reading my story.

Readers: YOU SHALL LIVE AND NOT DIE, BY HIS STRIPES YOU ARE HEALED AND YOU ARE FEARFULLY AND WONDERFULLY MADE.

Satan, I serve notice on you now, you are defeated—access denied! And God, we give You great praise. Have Your way in US and through US. In Jesus' name, I pray.

Amen.

The Fight of My Life

"Be still, and know that I am God: I will be exalted among the heathen,
I will be exalted in the earth."
Psalm 46:10

January, 2014 began what I believed to be a new and better year for me since the last two years were a little difficult. In 2012, I woke up from my sleep one night unable to move my neck from left to right; my entire body was stiff. The second time this occurred it was very painful, so I went to the doctor. He sent for an MRI of my neck and back. I went for my follow-up to get my results and he let me know that I had disc issues in my neck. He said I needed to see a spine specialist. Of course, the one he referred me to didn't take my health insurance, so my mom referred me to her office.

This doctor informed me that I had three bulging discs in my neck that were pressing against all my nerves on both sides, including my spinal cord. At times, it was impossible to turn my head to either side; I could barely walk. My arms, hands, and back were in constant pain because I couldn't and didn't want to take my medication as I should have. I knew that I still had to maintain my normal life and work.

Toward the end of January, 2014, I woke up one morning to feel and see a knot on my chest. It was hard and painful to the touch. I went to show it to my mom and asked her for her opinion. "Ma, look...feel it, what do you think it is? That's not normal is it?" Of course, she said, "I don't know what it is; I'm not a doctor. Go get it checked."

After a couple of weeks, I still hadn't seen my doctor. My mom would ask me at least once a week if I called. By this time, it was the middle of February. I still hadn't gone to the doctor. The knot was still there and painful to the point that I couldn't sleep comfortably.

One day while at work sitting at my desk, I received a text: "DID YOU CALL THE DOCTOR?" OH MY GOD! UGH! I thought. This woman is about to drive me crazy. Let me call this doctor. My appointment was scheduled for a few days later. The doctor checked and, after seeing and feeling the knot, he said, "I don't think it's anything but we'll send you for a mammogram. It's probably just a cyst." I scheduled my mammogram for the following week. I told my mom about the appointment and that the doctor didn't think it was anything.

On the day of my mammogram, I signed in and they called my name. I went to get undressed and go into the imaging room. After about the fourth picture, I was crying because of the intense pain of the machine pushing down on my breast and the knot. When I began to cry, the woman taking the images kept apologizing but stated that they had to get more images of the breast as far back as they could, against the breast wall. Anytime I needed to take a break, I could just let her know and she would stop, but I wanted it over so I just cried and kept going. After about fifteen shots, they finally got all the images they needed. It felt like an hour of intense torture.

I also had to get a sonogram of my breast. Usually sonograms are painless, but for me, it was painful every time they went around the knot in my breast. I watched on the screen as they were doing the sonogram and I could see it. It was actually kind of cool to see. On the screen it was a small, black, odd-shaped mass. After they took all the images for the sonogram,

I was taken back to get dressed, then I had to go and see the radiologist who looked at my images.

When I walked into the room, my images were up on the monitor. The radiologist said, "What I can tell you is that's not a cyst. You need to get a biopsy done." Most people would have panicked at that moment, but I didn't. I knew that Hebrews 13:5 says, "Let your conversation be without covetousness; and be content with such things as ye have: for he hath said, I will never leave thee nor forsake thee."

The next day I called my gynecologist to schedule my follow-up. I got an appointment for the very next day. My gynecologist had the results from my mammogram. He said, "I think it's probably just fibroids, but you need to see a breast surgeon." I called and scheduled an appointment for the following week. I thought I was just going for a consultation but when I got there, the surgeon did his own exam and sonogram.

After seeing the mass himself, he said we could do the biopsy that same day. I immediately got nervous because: 1) I wasn't prepared and 2) I don't like needles, but I agreed because I wanted it over with.

I returned to the waiting area to let my son know they were going to do the biopsy. I went back into the room and they began to prep me for the biopsy. One woman was in the room to do the sonogram so the doctor would know exactly where to go with the needle. My surgeon told me to watch the screen and keep my head turned toward the monitor. He talked me through the entire process. He told me when he was about to numb the area. I felt a pinch and I could see the needle as it went in on the screen.

I was so amazed that I could see everything on the monitor

and that the needles didn't hurt as bad as I thought they would. After he numbed the area he said, "Okay, you're going to feel pressure and a loud noise but it won't hurt." I was still nervous because I didn't know what to expect even though he tried to explain. He told me to keep looking at the monitor and I would be able to see what he was doing.

The surgeon warned me that he was about to begin the biopsy. I heard the loud pop; I jumped. About three or four strips of the mass were taken during the biopsy. After the biopsy was finished, I had to speak with the nurse practitioner. She let me know they should have the results within three days and that, as soon as they received the results, she would call me.

She asked if I wanted to get the results over the phone and, if so, if it was okay to leave a message if I didn't answer the phone. The entire staff, including my surgeon, made me feel comfortable and they made sure I knew they were there for me. The mass was about 1.1 cm before the biopsy.

Three days later, my phone rang as I sat at my desk at work. The nurse practitioner said, "Hi Kelly, I have your results. Are you able to talk?" I said yes, of course. All the while my heart was pounding. "Honey, I am so sorry but your results came back positive.

You have breast cancer." She asked if I was okay because I was silent; I told her I was fine. She tried to assure me that the entire staff would be there for me every step of the way. I actually took it very well. I was quite calm. I didn't cry because it didn't come as a shock. I knew the moment I saw and felt the lump. After we hung up, I called my mom immediately but she didn't answer her phone. Later on that day, once everyone was home, I told her and my son.

All of the testing and blood work seemed to go slowly after that. I began to get frustrated because I was still working and taking care of home and family in between getting tests done. I felt like I had tests every week; more than once a week it seemed I was in a doctor's office. I worked up until the day before my surgery.

On April 9, 2014, I went into the hospital to have a lumpectomy along with the removal of a few lymph nodes. I thought this process was going to be a breeze because the surgery went well and the recovery wasn't painful. But on Wednesday May 7, 2014, I began the most painful, uncomfortable, and weary process I ever had to endure: chemotherapy.

I will NEVER forget that day. I was nervous because I didn't know what to expect, but I was also excited because I was ready for the entire process to be over. My cousin and aunt went with me. When I got to the office, they gave me a pill for nausea then I was injected with five big syringes of the chemo medication. Two syringes were red and the rest were clear.

The first one they injected into me made me sleepy immediately. As soon I was injected with the red medicine, I immediately lost my sense of taste. When I got home, I went straight to sleep. I lost my appetite and, even when I tried to eat, I couldn't taste anything. I didn't want to drink anything.

All I wanted to do was sleep. It took me two days to drink one bottle of water. By Friday, I felt like I was dying. I became weak, could barely eat or drink, had severe pain, barely had strength to walk, and my bedroom was all the way on the top level. By Saturday, I started having diarrhea; that made me even weaker because I still wasn't eating. By Sunday, I felt like my life was at the end and I had nothing left.

I was ready to give up, call it quits, and not do another treatment because it was so hard and painful. I cried every day and night, unless my children were around. I refused to let them see me weak in the flesh. I tried to keep a positive attitude when they would come around but, little did they know, I was broken and hurting on the inside. I cried throughout most of the chemo treatments because my oncologist never gave me any pain medication.

It didn't matter how many times I would tell them I was in pain. They would tell me to take Tylenol and I would tell them that it didn't work, and still, no prescription. I was able to get pain medication only after I went to my primary care physician, toward the end of my chemo treatments. By then, I could barely walk. It seemed that during the week, when I had to get my treatments, that's when I felt like no one was around. I felt alone while everyone else went on with their lives and I struggled.

I began chemotherapy on May 7, 2014 and had my last treatment on September 10, 2014. During my first treatment, I needed to talk to someone. On the Sunday right after my treatment, I tried to think of who I could call because I felt so awful, but I remembered that everyone was in church. And then, my phone rang. It was one of my aunts, who is more like a sister to me. She asked how I was doing and I just broke down in tears.

As I cried, I said, "This is just so hard and I don't know if can do this." I know that when she called she hadn't expected to hear me crying but, when she did, she immediately started to pray and intercede on my behalf. After she prayed, she said that if she could take my place she would, but God knows which battles to give to whom. She told me to think of the story of Job in the Bible.

He was stripped of everything yet he never faulted God nor did he ever talk badly about God. He remained faithful. She said just think of the people that you will help, people that will come to Christ because of your testimony of how God healed your body. It felt so good to have someone to talk to and pray me through right on time.

I finally started to feel a little better and a little more strengthened by Tuesday. I was thankful because I only had to have chemotherapy every other week for the first four rounds. They were injected into my medical port and only took about five minutes.

The last four rounds had to be given every twenty-one days; those treatments took about an hour. Going through chemotherapy was a very difficult and trying time because I felt helpless. I was weak, and it became hard to care for my children and hard to walk.

Every step I took was painful. It hurt to stand. I could barely bathe myself because I couldn't bend to sit in the tub and it hurt to stand long enough to take a shower. It was painful to bend, dress myself, and tie my shoes. I would cry when I had to walk up the stairs. My feet, ankles, and legs stayed swollen. My last chemo treatment was on September10, 2014 and I had to do radiation from October to November.

Throughout the whole process, I went to church every chance I could and praised my way from the beginning to the end of my endurance. It wasn't until after my endurance and I was cancer free that the devil attacked me again. This time it wasn't through my body; he began to attack my mind.

I became seriously depressed and even thought about suicide. I stopped going to church, stopped praying, stopped reading the Bible, and never reached out for help. I felt so alone and felt like no one cared because no one called to check on me, not even to see why I hadn't been in church lately. When family would call, I would lie and say I was fine. If they asked why I hadn't been in church, I would tell them I was tired to cover the fact that I was really depressed, suicidal, and didn't want to go into the house of the Lord in fear that someone would see that I was dying mentally.

It became so bad that I thought about taking all the medication I had sitting next to my bed. I knew that that would kill me for sure. The only thing that made me fight against my mind was looking my babies in the face.

I would think, who would take care of them if died? How would they handle me not being here to care for them to watch them grow? Just the fear of knowing the pain they'd be in because of me, I couldn't kill myself. But that was my daily fight. The devil kept telling me that they would be better off, and reminded me of how difficult life was due to the aftermath of cancer treatment.

Bills had piled up and, even though I was back at work full-time, I was still struggling financially. Many times I could not put food on the table, pay my light bill or gas bill, and I struggled to pay car payments and car insurance. On top of that, I had my little ones in school and didn't have the money for everything the school requested.

I felt like I was at my lowest point. One day, after months and months of not going to church, one of the pastors from my church called me and said she wanted to see me back in the house. She reminded that me that so many people hadn't made it through cancer, but God healed me from it. Before we got off the phone she prayed for me.

The whole time she was on the phone I was crying because I was at a very low place and so depressed, but after that call I started going back to church. Even though I started going back to church, I felt out of place because the devil still had my mind. Satan had me to believe that I wasn't good enough, I was damaged goods, God had no use for me, nobody cared, and it wouldn't matter if I was no longer here.

I would go and sit there and not even lift my hands to give God praise. The devil had me so bound that I was ungrateful and felt as if I had no reason to live because even though I was finished with my cancer treatment, I was still physically and mentally suffering and no one asked if I was okay.

But one Sunday, I got up early and got ready for church; I was even at the car first, waiting for my son who is always waiting for me. From the very beginning, service was intense. My Bishop was on fire. He went around praying and prophesying to people, and then he went back to the pulpit. The spirit of God was in there! Out of nowhere, I heard him say, "Kelly stand up."

I stood and he told me to raise both hands and begin to tell God "Thank You." He told me that God healed my body from cancer and reminded me that not everyone makes it through what I've been through. He said that I'd become depressed and that that was because I hadn't surrounded myself with those who pray. Bishop said every time I gave God thanks, it should get louder and louder.

My oldest daughter was standing next to me and my son was standing in the row in front of me. I remember Bishop told him to go to me and pray me through as I began, as he was the one who went through the process of cancer with me; he was in the house and saw firsthand what I had to endure and what God allowed me to conquer.

At that moment the spirits of depression and suicide broke off of me. I began to cry out louder and louder, saying "Thank You!" to God for healing me. I began to tell God "Yes! Yes, to Your will! Yes, to Your way!" as my son was praying for me.

I fell to the floor. Bishop told people: "Pick her up! She's been lying around long enough!" He told them to bring me to the front and then he told me to praise God. I began to shout and praise God with tears streaming down my face.

As I was shouting, I could hear my Bishop say, "I wonder what are all of those around her gonna do!" The next thing I knew my oldest daughter, who was still in her seat, was in the front with her arms around my waist, shouting with me! That day is when I knew, without a shadow of a doubt, God is real and He is a deliverer, if we just believe. Ask me how I know—HE DID IT FOR ME!

I wrote a part of my story with the hope that it will encourage someone to keep fighting. You shall live and not die! Although the process is uncomfortable and uneasy, just know that you're in your "Walk Through" season. You've just read the story of someone with bulging discs pressing against all the nerves on both sides of her body, endure and conquer stage two breast cancer, surgery, chemotherapy, and radiation. Guess what? I'm still here!

If you've ever wondered, do miracles really exist, you just read about one! Who did it? God did!

—

LOOK OUT FOR THE CONTINUATION OF THIS
TESTIMONY!

Questions for Reflection

1.   At some point we've all had the experience of being surrounded by others but still feeling alone. I dealt with it by abandoning the church and pretending everything was okay. Learning from my example, how would you handle this experience going into the future? What are some things you can do? Who in your life can you reach out to?

_____

_____

_____

_____

_____

_____

_____

2. Do you know what your purpose is in life? If so, how can you better handle the dark days when a voice tells you that it's okay to give up? What scriptures can you speak into your life to combat the forces of darkness that would have you give in to your fears? If you aren't sure of your life's purpose, what are some steps you can take, besides praying and fasting, to begin finding out what it is?

_____

_____

_____

_____

_____

_____

_____

CHAPTER THREE

Sonia's Prayer

Dear Lord, my savior and my best friend: I pray that readers will get a sense that You make us promises and You keep them. You stick closer than a brother; You are dependable, faithful, and loving. You do not give us what You know we can't handle. I hope they will see that faith in God, determination, praising Him and thanking Him before they even get the answer to their prayers will keep them focused and build their faith. If any of them have not given their heart to You, I pray You convict them so they can have salvation and eternal life. Praise the Lord Jesus.

AMEN.

My Life Is in God's Hands

"Fear thou not; for I am with thee: be not dismayed; for I am thy God: I will strengthen thee; yea, I will help thee; yea, I will uphold thee with the right hand of my righteousness."
Isaiah 41:10

I am a woman of destiny, living out Your plan, knowing where You'd have me walk, being guided by Your hands. Proverbs 14:1 states: "Every wise woman buildeth her house: but the foolish plucketh it down with her hands."

I was born in the West Indian island of Jamaica. My mother and stepfather migrated to the British Isles, England when I was a young girl. I have one younger brother, and a sister, who passed away in 2013.

Growing up, I had mixed feelings because my parents were very strict disciplinarians. I thought I was not loved because of this. I did not know then they were grooming me for the outside world. I was born with an incurable eye condition called retinitis pigmentosa. I made sure that it did not prevent me from being a normal person. I did not like the word "disabled" so I tried every chance I got to educate the public about my eye condition.

I observed how they addressed me and I wanted them to understand there was nothing wrong with my brain. I was visually impaired but I functioned just like any other person— 100%—with accommodations. The condition leaves pigmented areas (dead areas where there are no light sensitive cells in my retina), so no light gets into the cells. This makes it difficult to see, especially at night; I also have no peripheral or side vision. Night blindness was one of the symptoms. As a child, I thought I was just clumsy because, in school, I was always falling and bumping into things. I went BANG! into a glass door. It looked like it was open. In high school, I started to do college work with permission from my parents and Principal Byfield. I remember his name to this day; he was a very kind man.

I used to say I wished the world was always lit up with lots of light, then I would not have to depend on anyone. I could not go anywhere by myself: no movies, no social gatherings, no visits to anyone's home. If I decided to go somewhere by myself, I had to take a cab. I had to let the person know that I was coming and let them know when I was leaving my house, so they could time it and meet me downstairs. In high school, I knew I would have to sit in the front of the class because I couldn't see the blackboard.

I learned to speed write and make friends with a few students, so that if I missed anything I could ask for assistance. Otherwise, I would ask if I could tape the speaker. We were asked in school what we wanted to major in. I chose ophthalmology because of my condition. In England at that time, one would go one day per week for six weeks to a place where the profession you wanted would be so that you could see if you really liked it.

This gave you a chance to change your mind before you chose your major for college. I chose the eye infirmary because my mother worked there at that time, and I was fascinated by eyes.

One day in the operating room with the surgeon, while assisting him, I said, "Sir, I don't see in the dark like other people."
"No one sees in the dark," was his response.

I said I noticed that my eyes did not adjust like others did. He told me to come to his office during break time and he would have a look at my eyes. When I got there, he said, "You're right. I see something in the back of your eyes, the retina; I'll give you a letter to take to the ophthalmologist." I was told I had this hereditary disease. My father and his brother had it. My father died in 1989 on Christmas Eve.

He was a much respected man, a deacon in the church for many years. It was very pleasing to my ears to listen to the tributes from the young people. He always used to write to me, telling me about the things of God. I only knew that he lost his sight in both eyes after he died; they didn't want to tell me. They hid it because they knew I had the same problem.

My teenage years were wonderful. I received the Lord into my heart at the age of ten in Sunday school. During my teen years, I was a faithful and happy steward for the Lord's work. I first joined the church choir. I later became the treasurer for the Sunday school, then the church reporter. Finally, I became a Sunday School teacher. I enjoyed teaching the children. I had lots of ideas in my head and I utilized them. After many years, I became the youth leader. I used to organize many banquets at the end of the year; all the young people from the New Testament Church of God would come and they would exchange phone numbers. Eventually, some even got married. At that time, I was into drama and looked forward to the Youth Convention. I was very busy for the Lord, always doing His work and enjoying it. My unsaved friends would ask me if I wanted to go to secular gatherings, and I'd tell them no.

During my early 20's, I could not date like my counterparts; my mother was very strict. At twenty-six years old I met my first boyfriend. He eventually became my husband. You may say, "How did you know he would be your husband?" I knew he was sent to me from the Lord. We met in church at a wedding. My cousin's girlfriend invited me. Every time I turned around, I caught him looking at me and smiling.

I remembered seeing that face on a portrait somewhere but I could not remember where. It turned out that I had taught his younger brother in Sunday School. He was giving his mother some trouble and they had asked me to come to the house to talk to him. That is where I had seen the portrait on the wall. At the time, I did ask who that handsome young man was. I had also gone to school with his younger sister Joan. He was very handsome, but it was not the looks that got me. He was a gentleman indeed: polite, respectful, helpful, and kind. He would ask me if I needed anything and I would say no, but he would always bring groceries to the residence.

We were engaged for one year. When he proposed to me, I did not hesitate. I gladly said, "Yes! Yes! Yes!" But in the back of my mind, I was very scared. You see, none of my relatives or friends thought I would ever get married. It was going to take a miracle or I'd be a "nun" forever. But we married on November 13, 1976. It was a foggy morning, which made me apprehensive. I was thinking about the photos, but it turned out to be a glorious day. I was never interested in boys; I thought they were immature, but the boys in my church always came to me for advice.

They said I was very serious and not "giggly" like the other young girls. His mother and I got along fabulously from day one. We were like sisters and throughout the marriage she was very supportive. Once, I had a surprise birthday party for her. She told her best friend that I was the only person who made her feel like a human being. We had a wonderful wedding with 100 guests, but I was a little sad because my mother could not come. She was in Tennessee as she did not have her green card.

On the honey moon night, we were in Paris—the most romantic city in the Western hemisphere. But I was scared and nervous. I started thinking, I've never been so close to the opposite sex! What am I going to do? I was becoming overwhelmed; I truly didn't know what to expect. We went out for a meal when we got to the hotel, strolled around the city, and saw the Eiffel Tower.

It was time to go to bed. I panicked, went to the bathroom to shower, and refused to come out. This must seem very funny, but it happened. When he asked me what was wrong, I said, "This is not a cliché. I have a terrible headache." He was kind to me, trying to calm me down, but I would not come out. Eventually, I fell asleep in the bathroom. I felt someone pick me up and place me on the bed. He left me to sleep and I thought, how many men would be so kind and gentle? I respected him for that. I loved him even more.

Years passed by and I realized that I did not have to ask him to do anything in the house—it would be fixed before I asked. When I cooked, he washed the dishes, clean the pots and the stove, mopped the kitchen floor, and took out the garbage. I know he loved me very much and I loved and respected him. We would discuss everything. I would validate him and he would validate me, and we would compromise in the middle.

I remember when he gave me his entire pay, I gave it back to him. I said, "Take up your responsibilities and I will do mine." That was the only discussion we had about finances. When the car note and the insurance bill arrived, I would just step in and help him without a problem. He was a homebody but very spontaneous.

Seven years later, I got pregnant and had a handsome baby boy. I looked at him and said, "Welcome into the world.

You are here for a purpose." I kid you not, he smiled at me. No one believed me; they said it was gas, everything except a smile.

All throughout school, they called him "Smiley" because whenever he wanted something he would smile. The day I came out of the hospital with him, I took him to the church and said to the pastor, "I know that this is not customary but I would like you to bless my son." He agreed, and then everybody took the baby so I could enjoy the service. His father was amazing. Sometimes he would say, "Pack a picnic basket, call our son's friend, and tell his mother we are taking them to Rye Playland." That became our favorite place.

As our son grew up, he became a hardworking young man. He had three jobs while in high school and they did not affect his schoolwork. He has a great personality and is loyal to friends and family. He is now a father for the first time at thirty-three years old, the same age I was when I had him.

Look out for Volume 2!

Questions for Reflection

1.   Reflect on two separate occasions when you knew that your life was "in God's hands."

_____

_____

_____

_____

_____

2.   List three blessings in your life that you take for granted below. Resolve to more mindfully give praise and thanks to God for them.

_____

_____

_____

_____

_____

CHAPTER FOUR

Zavier's Prayer

Allow me to recognize in desperate times, oh Lord, that experiences both plentiful and suffering will bring me closer to You. Being a credible witness of the wealth of your love for mankind, I hope to inspire others toward the beauty of the faith. I pray Father that as the pages of my own life turn over, You remind me of the bigger picture. I pray that my attitude turns from stone and develops into a gentle tone that others may hear the love in my words and identify me as Your child, a vessel of strength and hope in a misguided world. May Your amazing spirit come in and feel at home in our hearts.

Amen.

Trust on Your Mark

"Though I speak with the tongues of men and of angels, and have not charity,
I am become as sounding brass, or a tinkling cymbal."
I Corinthians 13:1

Cheerless, the joy for Nicholye didn't come. He stared at the broken glass that covered the streets as he walked in from school. Trembling all over, his thoughts yelled through his mind. I should've trusted my instincts! I knew that guy in the hallway was up to something.

Earlier that morning, he had felt a coldness run through him as he ran down the stairs, heading to school, but he ignored it. He was too busy rushing to catch up with Dominic and Mikey before the first bell rang. Beverley, his mother, wasn't just any mom. She had the enduring elements of a lioness, brave and strong, ready to devour for her young.

Though she could only see dimly out of her right eye, the vision of greatness was upon her and her cubs. She knew the potential her children had, and did everything she could to encourage them. That morning, she'd promised Nicholye, his brother Trevor, and sister, Ellie—a freshman to the school and envious of her older brothers' popularity—a new pair of sneakers.

Excited and expecting, Nicholye sat in class, counting down every second to every minute. In his mind, he matched up the gear that was going to compliment his new kicks. He had an unusual sight of things, visually sharp and mysteriously imaginative.

His old soul spent most of its leisure time reading books on social sciences, while his current generation struggled to find their paths. They were too preoccupied by sports, the internet, and feelings of lust. There was a lack of love and family structure in his community and this bothered Nicholye.

Although he was young, his soul was almost fully blossomed. Rather than be accepted, Nicholye wanted to reinvent a new way of being young, while living in the likeness of God. As to why this topic of love and human behavior inclined him so deeply at a time he felt he was too early in his life, was a question he constantly struggled with himself.

Yet, he trusted the path. Those that knew him was sure God put him up for a purpose. He was marked as God had elected. He often found himself conversing with those who were more seasoned, finding the wisdom in their conversations as nourishment to his divergent and unique way of thinking.

This skill allowed Nicholye to connect with different generations, giving him the knowledge necessary to see the big picture of life. "Nicholye!" He sat upright immediately at his desk with his hands folded. "What an idea, Ms. Fox. That was great!" The class laughed.

"The question was; why should we care about endangered species?" Nicholye responded in a humble tone and quoted, "Whoever is righteous should have regard for the life of his beast, for what happens to the children of man and what happens to the beasts is the same, as one dies, so does the other."

Ms. Fox stared searchingly in his face. "Impressive, Nicholye, would you like to further instruct the class on the subject of what the destiny of a student who has latent excellence but fails at paying attention to class material might be?" The aroused class adjusted their attention at him. With a charming expression on his face, one arm on his desk, the other holding his chin, he chuckled.

"I'm honored, Ms. Fox, but I'd prefer to prolong the youth of my fellow classmates as my teaching skills can be a bit life changing."

The dismissal bell rang. *** "I will not disrupt the class with stupidity," Trevor wrote tediously on the blackboard as he held the chalk, frowning in obvious disgust. Mr. Miller didn't want to see a portion of his blackboard dodged. Since Trevor had a fist-pumper attitude, he seldom would think things over before reacting, the impulsive side always landing him a seat in detention.

Nicholye left his class in search of his brother but quickly realized after waiting five minutes that if Trevor wasn't in the schoolyard, he was held back for something he did. As usual. It was well into midday, and all of the other students had been dismissed. Still, Mr. Miller held Trevor hostage until he felt the ransom of Trevor's defiance was dispatched.

Mr. Miller was a long-faced, unsmiling man who exercised discipline and expected nothing but exceptional obedience. He had been this way throughout all the years he instructed the class, and no one had the courage to go against him. Sure, some threw a fit about the way he conducted himself, but he was never challenged for his reputation.

Trevor grew annoyed and outraged, looking over the amount of what he wrote then gazing back at Mr. Miller sitting at the back of the class, motionless, with a face that seemed unsatisfied. The voice in Trevor's head mocked him. This guy won't quit.

You're in way over your head, so if you run now, how much worse could be in store for you on Monday? You'll come in and Mr. Miller will run over his usual lines to intimidate you then escort you to his quote unquote "palace of discipline".

Trevor glanced at the door. Though his inner righteous man planned to ignore the escape, his tired flesh was through and due for some kind of excitement. The classroom phone rang and Trevor used this moment to dash between the desks, running past Mr. Miller who sprang up in his confusion. But Trevor's athletic stature was gone with the wind, swooping through the halls.

Sunset was soon approaching by the time Nicholye saw his brother, and he threw his hands in the air, laughing. "Down in the cards, huh? Well, at least there was light at the end of that tunnel. Mr. Miller really has it out for you. I thought you weren't gonna make it out." Trevor grew even more dispirited at his brother's indirect concern.

With his head cast down, he quietly added, "Yeah, right more like the front lights of a train coming straight at me!" "Your biggest opponent is you, Bro. Every time you rebel, you put your back against the wall. Mom needs us to be the arms for her one day and that way out is knowledge." Trevor chuckled under his breath.

Frustrated at his brother, Nicholye took a deep breath before adding, "Hear me out, yo. On a more serious note, we're put at an obvious disadvantage! To escape being a statistic, we must rise above the standard in which the social condition is. Take a look around us; everyone we watched growing up fell into the same destructive cycle of addiction, hustling, and smuggling themselves into the prison pipeline."

—
35

As Nicholye's passion grew, he paused as if he envisioned himself empowering black prominence. His aspiration one day was to eliminate physical, mental, and spiritual bleakness to improve the context of living for blacks in America and abroad. Trevor thought to himself for a moment, but his esteem about his ability was far too slim. Beverley stormed out of the school with Ellie and spotted both of her sons in the schoolyard.

Since their father, Stephen had died from a failed heart transplant, it hadn't been easy for her and her children. They knew she could taste the worry in her mouth every trip to the grocery store, and often bit down on her lip while choosing which bills she would skip to keep them in blissful spirits since their father's untimely death. With barely enough resources, she still managed to dodge eleven evictions.

Once, they were just hours away from being escorted out by the city Marshall but their mom fell deeply in prayer, not allowing this defeat to become a reality. God, being inseparable to their family, heard all of her silent cries, sending His chariot once again. And before the sun had reached its highest, they were able to relocate unbothered and sheltered.

Trevor squinted his eyes quickly against his mother's fury as she stormed toward him. "Wait, Mom!" he screamed. "Wait, Mom!" he said again, eyes tightly shut, as if his eyelids could shield him from his mother's tongue lashing and rebuke.

Beverley grabbed him by the head and peered directly into the eyes of her firstborn son, powerfully drawing up all of her strength. "If you're too grown to conduct yourself in the halls of study then you're much too grown to live under my roof!

I've had it up to about the height of the good heavens!" Not feeling the earth beneath his feet, Trevor wiggled, trying to free himself from his mother's clutch, staring guiltily in every direction. Gathering his stance quickly, he realized that by being in the schoolyard, his friends could be watching. Beverley's volume dropped into her stomach, brewing up a fierce balance as she started to speak deeply yet as softly as a wise elder. "Listen to me.

God has ordained every being a great work for that being to satisfy himself in life. I will not let you grow to scatter this happiness in the wind. There will come the stage, son, when you've exalted into manhood and your world will shake you and try all that you know and test all that you've become; for you to ever have to bear in question whether you amount on the world's scale is what I dearly forbid.

So I need you to straighten out these disruptive episodes of aggression, harness it up with wisdom, use it instead as a desire to fight for greatness in life." It was evident that his mom looked upon her children as fallen stars from the heavens, and before she let the world repel that light, she was on a mission to make sure they were rightly viewed. Her faith would keep her and she knew she was in good hands.

Awakened by his mother's truth, there followed a moment of silence and Trevor felt a great well of peace in his heart. It overwhelmed him as he saw the loving patience in his mother's eyes. "Sorry, Mom. I shouldn't be this way; there is so much turmoil in my head ever since God called Dad and Erving back.

I've often felt so aroused in anger that everything I love in life will eventually slip away." Erving was a real close accomplice to Trevor. He suffered a great deal of depression, paranoid from the life he lived, stealing cars and boosting the parts to local car enthusiasts. There was a hit out on his life and where they lived that meant instant casualty.

—
37

Reassured by his conversation with his mother, he swore to himself to never stunt the many blessings endowed on his life. *** The shades of evening had begun to fall, the air cool, as they headed toward their block. Passing the first stretch of buildings where local thugs would bask in the shadows, there was a sudden air of unhappiness.

When they got to their building, they bypassed the faulty elevators, which often reeked of urine, and lugged over to the stairs. One by one, they took flight up to their fourth-story apartment. As they made it to the top, a great dark spirit came upon Nicholye's mind. He wasn't sure if it was just his pessimistic side or if something was truly wrong. He had been so focused on the sneakers that they had never gone to get. He looked at his mom, Beverley, who was now walking in front of them.

She would normally stay behind them as they walked, overseeing. Approaching the front door, she reached into her purse in search of her keys, but before she could put the key into the lock, she noticed the door slightly ajar. She paused, wondering if it was her doing then directed her children to stay behind her as she investigated.

Beverley was at loss for words. "Oh my God!" she said, as they looked upon what used to be their kitchen window…

TO BE CONTINUED…
Look out for the full book!

Questions for Reflection

1.   Who are the people in your life who you would consider your warriors, the people who have your back, support, and are honest with you? Do you honor them and show your love and gratefulness for their place in your life? If so, how? If not, how can you better honor them?

_____

_____

_____

_____

_____

2.   Think of someone you've greatly admired (a parent, pastor, former teacher/professor, etc.) What do you admire about them? What characteristics of theirs do you wish to imitate and why?

_____

_____

_____

_____

_____

_____

CHAPTER FIVE

Bevelyn's Prayer

Father, I come to You now in the name of Jesus. Thank You for all You have done for us. Thank You for providing us with everything we need to live. We appreciate Your goodness. I come, Father, asking You to forgive us of any sin we have committed against You. Help us to walk upright before You.

I come now on behalf of the one reading this chapter. Life has not been kind to them. The love they sought may not have been found. And now, they find themselves in the midst of depression. This is not the plan You had for them. This is not the life You designed for Your child. So now, Father God, I come asking You to strengthen Your child as only You can. I come against the spirit of depression in the life of whoever is reading this chapter. We bind that foul, demonic spirit in the name of Jesus. Depression, we demand you let this person go in Jesus' name! And it is so!

Amen!

Just One Word

"Why art thou cast down, O my soul? And why art thou disquieted in me?
Hope thou in God: for I shall yet praise Him for the help of his countenance."
Psalm 42:5

I don't know where to begin. There is so much I want to say and so much I'm not ready to share. I guess it's my pride or embarrassment, and the fact that I haven't told anyone else. I'm still afraid. Fear. My old "friend." The one that gets me into situations I don't belong in. The one that still haunts me and still taunts me. I can't move forward because of fear and I can't go back because of it. It seems I've been spinning my wheels all my life. I should have gotten my college degree back in the 70's, but fear made me quit school. I don't know what I was afraid of. Maybe I was afraid of success. Maybe I was afraid of failure. Either way, I dropped out after two years. I keep saying I'll go back; it's been thirty-something years now. I will go back. I will.

For two years, I stayed home and babysat my little sister and my niece, then I took a secretarial course. I learned the basics, but I wasn't very fast. I didn't have a typewriter at home to practice on. But I finished and got a certificate. I don't even know where it is now. Probably with a lot of my past. While I was in that class, I made a "friend." After all these years, I can't remember her name. Anyway, together we decided to go to the mall and apply for jobs. We applied at all the same stores, hoping we'd get hired at the same one. We didn't. She was hired at Alexander's; Macy's called me. We worked different schedules so that was the end of that friendship.

It is now 1979.

I'd been in and out of church for the past four years. My work schedule required me to work Sundays, so church was not an option. Now that I can't go, I want to go. Isn't that always the way? I really enjoyed my time at Macy's.

The older women taught me how to shop sales. Never pay full price, they said. Wait for it to go down. Been doing it pretty much like that ever since. Any young black man that came into our department was a potential suitor for me. They were always on the lookout for a nice young man for me. I loved those ladies. I often wonder how they are, if they are.

My manager, Georgette Pene (she was French), loved me like a daughter. I learned the value of hugging from her. She always had a hug or two for me. I could talk to her about anything. And she always gave me extra hours. Macy's had me on the books for thirteen hours. I always worked forty-plus hours and I always got the hours before the white girls. Ms. Penny, as we called her, was seventy then. I know she must be gone now.

So many days, I've wished she was still here to talk to. I resigned in 1986; she retired the following year after having worked for Macy's for over fifty years. Wherever you are, Ms. Penny, thank you so much! I love you dearly!

By the time I resigned, I had gone back to working part-time because the year before I got a full-time job working in an office. I got hired at a title company. This was the 80's and the housing market was booming! I started out as the receptionist; within a year I became the policy typist. When I think about it, I probably made more money back then than I do now! Anyway, in October of 1985, I decided to get back into church. I wasn't working Sundays anymore, so I had no excuse.

—

I had only been going to Kings Temple for maybe a month when Sis. Haywood asked if I would be willing to meet her friend. I asked who he was and she described him. She said he was one of the church's guitarists, and a minister. His name was Ben Monroe. With her description, I still couldn't figure out who he was. I didn't know a bass guitar from a lead guitar. Still don't.

We agreed to meet at her house for dinner about two weeks later. Still didn't know who he was. But I decided if he was a member, and this woman was willing to introduce us, what could it hurt? Hey, you never know—a lot of relationships started out as blind dates. Two weeks went by and I was at her house. He pulled up.

NOTHING LIKE I EXPECTED OR WANTED!

But I admitted, looks weren't everything. I wanted to see what he was about. "Get to know him," I said to myself. Maybe he is the one God has for me. Maybe he is the man of my dreams. We talked about ourselves, what we did, what we liked. You know, fluff stuff. I learned that he was a disabled vet and into music and was in the process of putting an album together.

I told him I was working two jobs, full-time and part-time. I told him I had my own car and my own apartment and that I wasn't looking to get married. (I was twenty-eight and I really didn't think marriage was in my future.) I did like the fact that he had plans. He wasn't just floating through life taking it as it came. He had dreams and aspirations and was willing to share it with someone. Possibly me.

I don't recall him ever taking me on a real date. You know, dinner or a movie. We always did things that had to do with his music: a concert to pass out flyers, a rehearsal, to someone's house for a meeting, never just the two of us alone together. I should have seen it. I missed the signs. I wasn't paying attention. But he was about doing something, trying to be somebody. And I was in the middle of that! I was there! In the middle of making things happen! Not on the outside looking in at everybody else! I was in the meetings! I was part of the decision-making! ME! And I was his girl!

All these years later, I've continued to ask myself how I let this happen. Why did I let this happen? I was the "smart one." I was the "bright one." That's what people kept telling me. As I write this, I understand. I didn't want to be on the outside looking in. I wanted to be a part of what was happening. There. I said it.

I admit it. I no longer wanted to be known as this one's sister, or that one's cousin. I wanted to be known for me! I wanted to be accepted for me. But I was still his girl.

And I still wasn't known for me. After about two months of concerts I never enjoyed because I was working, and meetings about his album and whatever else, he took me home one night. We were in the car talking and the next thing I knew his hand was on my breast. Don't know if it was intentional or not. At this point, it doesn't matter. One thing led to another, and our relationship became sexual. (If I knew then what I know now…)

I was five months pregnant when we got married. Did I have misgivings? Yes! Did I have concerns? Yes! But I grew up in a one-parent household and I didn't want to raise my child that way. I wanted it to have the best possible life I could give. I wanted my child to have better! Those things about his past he didn't want to share, why did it nag at me so? Was he hiding a deep dark secret? Should I run?

I knew on my wedding night that I had made a mistake. There I was, five months pregnant, and he insisted on sex because it was our wedding night! But I was stubborn and I was gonna see this marriage thing through. It would not end in divorce! I was gonna turn him around! I was gonna make him the man I deserved! I was gonna make him better! I was gonna love him enough to change him!

I quit my part-time job when I was about two months pregnant and had already started to bulge. I worked my full-time job until about two weeks before my due date. I was tired and huge. I retained water like I was a well! I couldn't wear shoes the last month of my pregnancy because of the swelling.

I had to wear bedroom slippers—in March! But I still had to carry out my wifely duties: cooking, cleaning, sex. No matter how I felt. He never inquired how I was feeling. He never asked if he could do anything for me. Never did anything spontaneously for me. Not that I remember.

I suffered with depression, starting at about my seventh month of pregnancy. He never cared that I was down. He never tried to cheer me up. He complained when things were not to his liking. I remember burning chicken once. He told me there was no reason that should have happened. All I had to do was watch the chicken. Never mind all the other meals that weren't burned. He never asked if I was okay.

He was so preoccupied with himself that he couldn't see I needed help! In March, I gave birth to a beautiful little girl! The nurses couldn't get enough of her. She was adorable. A little red thing with curly hair. And I loved her! But I was still depressed. I couldn't shake it. I started pulling out of it by Memorial Day. The summer was good. In February, 1988, I realized I was pregnant again. Fear gripped me! Was I gonna

---

46

be pregnant every year?

Then came the depression. Earlier this time.

On top of this, Ben decided to counsel four children: three girls and a boy, teaching them music, voice, and instruments. Every Saturday! Every. Single. Saturday! All. Day. Long. By the summer, I was crying every time I was alone. I didn't know why.

It seemed I was crying for no reason. And he didn't help. He didn't offer comfort. There was no compassion. If it wasn't about him, it wasn't important. I would ask him to just have the students over every other week or at least cut down the length of time they were there. He wouldn't have it!

I can still feel the pain I felt then as I write this. I was desperate. I needed a way out!

That's it! The pills! His sleeping pills! I will take them tomorrow when he leaves then my pain will be over!

I went to bed with a plan. This was a Wednesday night in August, three weeks before I was due. I will look for the pills when he leaves tomorrow. If I can't find them, then I will take the Drano under the bathroom sink. Either way, my misery will end.

Morning came and he was gone. I looked everywhere for those pills! They were everywhere just a few days ago! Now, when I really needed them, I could not find one! So, I went to the bathroom, knowing that this was a messy alternative. I bent down and, with my hand on the Drano, I heard a voice over my right shoulder.

"Do you want him to raise her?"

47

Huh?
"Do you want him to raise her?"

In that instant, I saw my daughter sitting on a couch; I could tell her spirit was broken. I answered the voice, "No. But you have to do something. I can't take it anymore."

The voice said, "Done."

I was strengthened with that one word.

Now things are gonna happen! I thought. I grew up in church, was in church most of my life, had had encounters with God I have yet to share.
But that one word saved three lives! Just one word— DONE!

TO BE CONTINUED.

Questions for Reflection

1.　Briefly reflect on a time when you ignored signs that you were going down the wrong path (in a relationship, career, family, your spiritual life). What did you learn from that experience?

_____

_____

_____

_____

_____

2.　Mental health is a seldom talked about issue, but it affects millions of people every day, many of whom never ask for or receive help. Think about a time when you were under severe mental distress. Did you ask for help? If not, how, specifically, did you make it through? What would you do differently if you could?

_____

_____

_____

_____

_____

CHAPTER SIX

Kavon's Prayer

Heavenly Father, in the name of Jesus, I come to you as humbly as I know how. I thank You for healing me from cancer. I believe in your miracles, therefore I am standing in the gap for my brothers and sisters who may need healing in their body from cancer or any other health issues. By Your stripes, we are healed!

In the name that is above every name.

Amen.

Lion's Roar

"And we know that all things work together for good to them that love God,
to them who are called according to his purpose."
Romans 8:28

My name Kavon Clayborn. I grew up in Roosevelt, New York.
I had a fairly normal childhood: I played with my brothers,
cousins, and friends. We rode our bikes and rollerblades, and
played the newest game systems. I just did the things that
regular kids would do, having no worries in the world.

I lived with my grandparents until I was a teenager, which
helped me build a very close relationship with them. In 2006,
they broke the news to the family that they would be moving to
Georgia; my mother, brothers, and I were moving to Islip, New
York. I was torn apart and my world had been turned upside
down. I was afraid; I didn't know what life was going to be like
for us without our grandparents around.

We moved to Islip when I was fifteen, and my grandparents
were on their way to Georgia. It was so painful to me. When I
laid in my bed, I would think, I am going to buy that house
back when I get older. That address was all I knew; it felt as if I
was in mourning.

My brothers and I attended Islip High School. I didn't really
care for the school at first, but I managed to deal with it
because I had my "ride or die"—my two brothers. By the end
of the year, I began to warm up to my new school.

I was now seventeen years old. One day, in gym class, our
assignment was to run around the one-mile track. Suddenly, I

became extremely tired and out of breath. I didn't mention it to anyone, not even my mother. I figured I was just tired from lack of sleep and, like so many of us, out of shape.

In the summer of 2007, I had the opportunity to visit my grandparents. While there, I found myself in the emergency room quite a few times. They gave me antibiotics; it didn't help at all. I kept getting nose bleeds. By the time my grandmother was able to follow up with the doctors, it was time for me to return to New York for school. When the school year began, I was in the eleventh grade.

The nosebleeds continued, so I finally gave my mother more details about the health issues I'd been experiencing, and suggested going to the doctor. She was dealing with her own health issues; I hadn't wanted to burden her until absolutely necessary.

I was in school for only three days and already I had a doctor's appointment. My mother was right on it! Because of the excessive, chronic bleeding, the doctor advised that I had to have a biopsy to determine the cause of my symptoms. It showed that I had a rare form of cancer called nasopharyngeal carcinoma, cancer of the sinuses. However, my doctor wasn't the one who told me.

I vividly remember my sister and aunt coming to my house. They, along with my mother, told me that I had cancer. I was completely in shock, to say the least.

My family took me to Memorial Sloan Kettering Cancer Hospital in New York, with the help of my cousin. I didn't know what to expect but I knew that I wanted to live; there were no other options. Since I was still considered a child (at the age of 17), fortunately, I was able to receive treatment in the pediatric unit, which was truly a blessing from God. The doctors at Memorial Sloan Kettering were so kind—they made the process more manageable for me. I remember when the doctors first evaluated me. They told me that I had stage 4a cancer. (I was told that stage 4b was the last stage.)

The doctors expressed that, considering all, I was doing pretty well. After the first evaluation, I began months of both chemotherapy and radiation treatment. This was all new to me but I knew that I had to go through the process because dying was not an option for me. During this time, my mother was also experiencing illness but she would always encourage me and tell me that I was a lion and lions roar. This always made me feel better (my mom passed away in 2008 and in her memory I now have a lion tattooed on my chest).

My family members were extremely supportive to me during this difficult time in my life and I am truly grateful for their love. I received a clean bill of health in March of 2008; I was so happy that words couldn't express how I felt inside. I am grateful that my mother was able to witness my healing (as she always prayed for me and had the type faith that can move mountains). I was heartbroken and devastated when my mom died just two months after I was told that I was cancer free. My mother died on May 8, 2008 (this is a day that I will always remember).

Sometimes, I ask myself why did God heal me and allow me to live but my mom died. I realize that I will never know the answer to this question but I do know that God knows exactly what He is doing (and for that, I am grateful).

I am now twenty-six years old and I take my health and fitness very seriously. I realize that I was given a second chance to live my life and nothing will hinder me from reaching my goals.

My new passion in life is to help others see the importance of eating healthy and exercising. I think many people take life for granted and it is only when you are faced with losing your life that you begin to honor the gift of life that God provides. I one-day hope to open my very own fitness center and train people in the area of health and fitness.

I have confidence to know that God will allow my dreams to come true, as He has allowed me to have another chance at life.

MORE TO COME!

Questions for Reflection

1.   How are your trials and tribulations connected to your purpose?

_____

_____

_____

_____

_____

2.   One of the many things we take for granted in life is family; for there are many people in this world who have had their biological family taken away or have been used, abused, and neglected by them. Use this space to reflect on the ways in which your family (however you define that) is both blessed and a blessing to you.

_____

_____

_____

_____

_____

_____

CHAPTER SEVEN

Tonya's Prayer

Heavenly Father, I thank You for Your daughter or son as they read this book. Father, I ask that my story gives someone courage who is in a hard place right now, no matter what their situation may be. Father, become their shelter and protector from all dangers and life's fears. I thank You that as You delivered and healed me, You will do the same for my sister or brother. Give them the ability to forgive others and themselves. I pray Your healing hand does the work. Give them courage, wisdom, and the peace of God to move forward and know that they are priceless in Your eyes. Do not allow the devil to keep them in any situation that is dangerous. Most of all, let them want to know who You are more than anything. In Jesus' name.

Amen.

What's Love Got to Do with This?

"Therefore if any man be in Christ, he is a new creature:
old things are passed away; behold, all things are become new."
2 Corinthians 5:17

My name is Tonya Jackson, and I've been broken by relationships. We learn how to love and be loved from our parents—how they love us, how they love each other, and how they love others—but when your foundation is unsure or incomplete, it can have you lost, dazed, and confused. When you lack guidance, you can quickly begin tumbling too fast down the wrong road. Yes, I was broken, but God never forgot me. This is my testimony.

From the age of six years old, I knew my mother was different. My first memory of her is the trips we took back and forth to the hospital, even though she didn't have any physical ailments. Sometimes my mother would take my sister and me on the bus and just go.

As a young child, I didn't really understand, but I grew up to know that my mother was diagnosed with schizophrenia. As a child, you know something is wrong but you can't put it into words; you just know that's she's very different from the other mommies.

As I got older, things became difficult. It was embarrassing to deal with a mom who was mentally unstable. So much so, that as a teenager, I would laugh at her absurdities. It was pain that I only knew how to soothe with laughter, as wrong as it was.

My father wasn't around. In fact, I barely saw him, so we were raised solely by a woman with a mental illness. I knew my mom loved me, but it was in her own way; not in the way that I needed as a young girl. She did the best she could, dealing with her own sickness, and I'll be eternally grateful for that, but it wasn't enough.

It was then that the enemy tried to plant those first seeds in my life. I tried so hard to be the complete opposite of my mom, but I ended up just like her in many ways, dealing with depression, near-breakdowns and other mental instabilities.

Without a father or, in many ways, a mother, I was drawn to seek out someone to love me, but it was the wrong kind of love. Searching for what I thought was love, instead I found: lust, betrayal, abuse, disappointment, hurt, and pain. After dating a "nice guy," I found the young man who I thought would love me. He was the stereotypical "bad boy"—a drug dealer, but to me, he was appealing. The relationship lasted about four years, but he was not at all who I thought he would be.

It started, as always, with a little push here, a little shove there. Then, as always, it escalated. He became possessive, and started beating me terribly, but I thought I was in love. He would wait for me to return from work and interrogate me for hours. Then he'd force me to smoke marijuana (which I hated) and perform sexual acts with him. If I didn't, he would beat me. One black eye, maybe two. He would threaten me by putting a loaded gun to my head, or inside my mouth. He had so many guns. He would always take me to isolated areas, so no one could be there to protect me.

Once, someone told him that I had been intimate with another man. He dragged me to his car and took off speeding; the car was all over the road. I was so afraid that we would get into an accident before he could get to his destination. He was in such a rage that he wasn't paying attention when we came to the drawbridge in Long Beach.

He didn't stop, ignored the gates, and over the open bridge we went. It's a miracle that we escaped that unharmed and I'm just grateful to God for keeping me, even in my mess. At this point, I could see he was taking me to what was then the Plantation Hotel—ironic name, isn't it? He always brought me there.

He got out, retrieved the keys to the room, and, in a rage, ripped off my white skirt and blouse. He grabbed the lamp, took out the bulb, and busted me in the lip with it. I was so afraid; I tried to run out of the room naked, but he caught me and forced me to perform sexual acts for the rest of the night. But that wasn't enough.

While we were at a birthday party at a local bar, I was dancing with his cousin. Nothing serious, just out having a good time. He saw me, grabbed me, and took me outside, a Moet bottle in his hand. Just as he was about to attack me with it, a friend saw us and took the bottle from him. Instead of shards of glass in my face and a possible trip to the hospital, he just gave me two black eyes that night.

While I was pregnant with Iesha, my first child, I asked a neighbor for a cigarette. When he found out, he walked me down the street and hit me in the mouth with a Heineken bottle, took me down to the Yankee Clipper Hotel and punched me in my stomach, knowing I was carrying his child. "I'm sorry. Why do you always make me do this to you!" he lamented when it was all over. That's what they always say. "Look at what you made me do!" You begin to question yourself. Maybe it is my fault.

At some point, I heard through the grapevine that he was cheating on me with another woman. We both lived in the same apartment building in the projects. He would go back and forth between us, abusing both of us at the same time. Sometimes, she even got it worse than I did. She had a mental breakdown and was admitted to a hospital. When I found out about her, we confronted each other. Both stubborn, we succumbed to "The Boy Is Mine" syndrome. It's funny how that works, isn't it?

Both beaten and treated as much less than we were worth, yet, we did all we could to hold on to him. We were in fear and in love at the same time. We were both pregnant at the same time; our daughters were born only a month apart. Despite our differences, we both vowed to never keep the children separated. Today, as young women, they are the best of friends, and so are we. We've become each other's strength. As for him…

When I decided to confront him, I thought I'd be slick. I went to his house and acted really nice so he'd let me in. He would often leave the house and be away for hours at a time, so when he left, I took the opportunity to get my revenge. I'ma fix him! I thought. I took his clothes and put them in a pile, grabbed a bottle of bleach, and went to town. But to my horror, he came right back!

He caught me and threatened me with one of his many guns. Then he broke a glass bottle and began to throw the pieces at me, cutting my face and body. He tortured me like this for hours, pointing his shotgun at me and telling me he'd shoot. I was petrified with fear; I thought for sure that I was gonna die that day. And all I could think was, Tonya, girl, what did you do? It was, of course, my fault.

These kinds of beatings went on and on. I would cry out to God and ask him what was wrong with me. My self-esteem was so low. I started out at about 160 pounds. I became 100 pounds soaking wet. I looked sickly and malnourished. My family and friends were so hurt and angry that I just kept dealing with the abuse. They couldn't understand the level of fear that was in me. They begged me to stay away from the monster that was doing this to me. I wanted to but the control that they have over your mind is indescribable.

One day, I just couldn't take it any longer. I finally got the courage to call 911 and had him arrested, but the system failed me as well. The same day he was arrested he was also released. He found me and cornered me that same night, threatening me once again.

My journey down the road of abusive relationships didn't end here, though; they just changed forms. Instead of physical abuse, I endured psychological, emotional, and sexual abuse. I came to believe that abuse was okay—it meant that he loved me. My image of what love is had become distorted. Eventually, I learned that I couldn't know what love is because I didn't love myself. But it would be a while before I truly understood that.

In the early 90's, I met the man who was the love of my life and would be the father of my two youngest daughters. We were more like the best of friends. I felt like I could share anything with him.

This was a big difference from my past relationships, where I felt like I couldn't freely express myself. I fell so deeply in love with him, but we were definitely unequally yoked. As many people think, though, I believed I could help change him, but he was never ready for that. I chose him because I'd hoped that finding someone tough enough to warn and scare off Iesha's father would help. The fear from my first relationship was still so real.

This one was never physically abusive, but he frequently cheated on me. I allowed this form of emotional abuse because my self-esteem still wasn't where it needed to be. God was slowly working on me, but I fell back into insanity—doing the same thing over and over, expecting different results.

After dealing with the constant cheating, not returning home some nights, finding out he had a child with another woman, I decided that I was tired of crying in God's ear, asking why I couldn't find someone to love me the way I needed and wanted to be loved.

I got pregnant. He told me to have an abortion or he would leave me. As hurtful and angry as I was, I did exactly as he said because I was afraid of losing him. He stayed and I continued to tolerate his infidelity. Again, I found myself pregnant, but this time I stood my ground. I told him that no matter what he said I was going to keep this baby, and I did. My second child was born in the mid-90s and she was the most beautiful baby.

During this time, we had many breakups and makeups. One night, I returned home and looked in my closet. He had packed his things and left. Not knowing where he went, I found out days later that he packed up and moved to Florida. No goodbyes to me or his baby girl; Ityra. Another bad boy.

Not long after he disappeared, I found out I was pregnant again. I didn't want him to know, but I told his mother, who still lived in the area. Of course, she told him. In hindsight, I don't know why I thought she wouldn't. He came back up to New York and, about a month later, Ivanna was born. She was a preemie.

He hung around for about a year, but he was always getting into trouble: robbing, stealing a dog from members of the

Italian mafia, and other mischief.

One day, around eight or nine in the morning, we both woke up. He said he was going to visit his mother. Around twelve, noon, I got a call saying that he was shot and killed. I had a premonition a week before that he would be taken from us. I looked over at him and he had this dead look to him—he literally looked dead. I know now that it was a death spirit, but I wasn't saved then, so I didn't know what it was. All I knew then was that one more tragedy had befallen me.

Amidst all this turmoil, I have always been grateful that, for all of her struggles, my mother gave my siblings and me the foundation of the church. After years of abuse, loneliness, and fear, I finally gave myself to Jesus in 2000.

I had been on the verge of a nervous breakdown. I finally surrendered and told God that I would go to church that Sunday. This was a Saturday. And wouldn't you know it, just like that ol' devil, he tried his best to sneak himself into my life, and cut off the plans that God had for me.

Right after I made the decision to go back to church, I received a call from my mother. I hadn't heard from her in a long while. She said, "What are you waiting for? Go ahead, break down!" Satan thought that those words would break me, but they only made me more determined—I knew it was him. The next day I went to church like I promised, and I got saved.

It was there that I met the man I would marry. It was a Sunday, and we had been checking each other out from a distance for a couple of weeks. One day, we struck up a conversation, talking about my car troubles. He told me that he worked on cars and gave me his number in case I ever needed help. He was serious, y'all—it wasn't a pick-up line!

Eventually, something happened to my car and I called him. He came over to my house to work on it for me. I was still leery because I had been through so much; my trust level was at an all-time low, but we started talking on the phone. We dated for a few months. It wasn't really butterflies and romance, feeling swept away. It was much more casual, but I could tell he was different. After a while, though, we had premarital sex.

One Sunday, our pastor's wife called us into the office. She'd had a dream that revealed to her that we'd been sleeping together. We admitted it, but the look on both of our faces showed we were mortified! How embarrassing and shameful! However, she didn't condemn us, but instead told us that God had us on His mind.

After this talking to from the leadership, I began to feel like he was shying away from me, like he was ashamed. I prayed, asking God for strength so that I wouldn't get hurt again, asking that He'd help me make the right decision, shield my heart and protect me. After a while, I got to speak to him. I told him, point blank, "You've been acting different. How about I go my way and you can go yours?"

His entire demeanor changed. He told me that I misunderstood him and that that wasn't how he felt. He said he loved me. After that, he began sending me flowers, he was always calling me, but I was already tuned out. I'd been hurt so much already. Eventually, he proposed to me. I told him no, straight up.

He would pour his heart out to me, but I decided that I would be really mean to him to see how serious he was. If he really loved me, I wanted to see how much he would take. I treated him so badly. As I look back on it, I realize that, for me, it was just a defense mechanism; he was getting the attitude that the men before him should've received.

He kept coming back, though, and kept proposing—three more times, in fact, and every single time that engagement ring got bigger. Finally, during that fourth proposal, I said yes. I figured if he was willing to go through all of that, he must really love me. He was such a gentleman with a big heart and a passion for God. He was a hard worker and the best stepfather anyone could ask for. Not only that, but he supported me in my various endeavors, getting my G.E.D. and my Associate's degree. We prayed together. He was the opposite of a bad boy.

We decided to transition to a new church, and our new pastor married us on August 29th, 2009, the biggest day of my life.

"What's Love Got to Do with This:
Part Two" Coming Soon!

Questions for Reflection

1.   What generational curses lie in your family (substance abuse, domestic violence, infidelity, child abuse, etc.)? List them here and "pray without ceasing" for their breaking. In addition, think of practical ways that you and your family can tackle these issues.

_____

_____

_____

_____

_____

2.   While we are all born in sin—none of us are "blameless" in God's eyes—there are some things in life that are not our fault, but the enemy would have us wallow in guilt. Think about and list below the uncontrollable things in your life that you may have blamed yourself for (domestic violence, sexual assault, tragic accidents, etc.) Then, in your prayers, tell Satan that he no longer has power over you and declare that you are free!

_____

_____

_____

_____

_____

CHAPTER EIGHT

Desiree's Prayer

Father God, in the name of Jesus, I humble myself in Your presence, giving You glory and honor for my sister or brother reading this book and my story. I ask that as my sister or brother reads the beginning of my story, they will be encouraged to see beyond their now and to go back and dream dreams again. I pray that they will have visions, write them down, and make them plain; believing and speaking boldly those things that are not as though they were, keeping an expectation for more in their spirits. For Your word says, You knew them before they were formed in the womb and that they are fearfully and wonderfully made. Father, I further ask, in the name of Jesus, that my sister or brother embrace the difference in them and know that because of this they are set apart for a purpose. You have plans for them, plans to prosper them and not hurt them, but to give them hope and a future. And, Father, in the name of Jesus, allow the writings in this book to speak a word into the spirit of those that may have found themselves led astray or far from Your peaceful shore, to return to their first love. Humble their hearts to forgive and receive forgiveness, to give their lives unto You, to call You Lord and Savior.

Amen.

Hidden Treasures: The Unfolding

"But as for you, ye thought evil against me; but God meant it unto good,
to bring to pass, as it is this day, to save much people alive."
Genesis 50:20

I can remember as a little girl—I'd say about eight or nine years old—going to my Uncle Andrew and Aunt Josephine's church, Lambert Chapel. Oh, how I sat in those pews listening and watching the Rev. Dr. Josephine Antley in awe as she walked, talked, and laughed in the pulpit. I didn't know it was preaching as I know it now.

Even now, I can almost hear her voice, see her face as if she were standing right here in front of me today. I wanted to be like her, look like her, talk like her, sound like her, and capture the attention of people like she did. She made you think...she made you dream!

She was polished, well spoken, smart, wise, intelligent, and beautiful! Her eyes sparkled all the time and she had a smile that would brighten the darkest day. And let me not forget: stern, strong, uncompromising.

No pushover, yet always a lady. Yes! I wanted to be like her, like all those things... yet? How did I get to this place? What did I do to deserve this? This is not the life I dreamed about. That I hoped for! No...this isn't it! Somehow, somewhere, I lost them: my confidence, my self-esteem, my smile, my joy, and my dreams. I'll get back to my opening title a little later.... Here I am, cleaning old people's apartments for a living. "Housekeeping specialist" is what it was called at one time.

However, they have stepped up into the big leagues—we're "homecare specialists" now.

I started this line of work because of my Great Aunt/Godmother. She had suffered a stroke some years ago (I was about ten years old) that left her paralyzed on her left side, arm, and leg. She wasn't able to walk without a cane; she had to wear a leg brace when she went out.

A few women had been assigned to her, to clean and cook for her, help administer her medication and so on, but for whatever reason, they all seemed to take advantage of her. People working in this line of work should have humbled hearts and compassionate dispositions; sadly, most do not.

I learned the hard way what the elderly must contend with when dealing with people that do not have a heart or the passion for helping those that cannot do or that are limited from doing things for themselves. Anyway, she had asked me to go down to her agency and apply and say that she had recommended me, which was true.

However, because she wanted me to work with her, I wasn't supposed to reveal our family relationship to anyone. So I agreed and went down there and filled out an application, but for some reason or another (I knew at the time but I don't recall it now), I wasn't selected to work hands-on with the elderly. I was informed that instead I could work in the home and be an escort of sorts when they needed to attend doctor's appointments, shop, and run errands. At first I was a little apprehensive about it because I just knew I was going to be working with someone I knew and was familiar with. Now all of that had changed and I had to go into some neighborhoods that were unsavory even for me (at the time I was in the 'hood myself). But being a young woman new to the surroundings, it wouldn't be hard to notice a stranger or "new jack" on the scene.

I remember once, I was sent to a client that lived in Coney Island. The buildings were tall, at least fifteen stories or more and the client didn't have a phone. Only one elevator in the building was working at the time and there were a few brothers hanging out in front of the building and in the building's lobby.

Needless to say, I was very apprehensive about this case here! I went into the building, got on the elevator, and pushed the floor I was heading to. The elevator had made two stops before getting to my floor; one for someone getting off and the second stop was for someone to get on. Low and behold, he was one of the same dudes that I had seen downstairs hanging out in the front of the building when I walked up!

I felt a little warm; I started sweating, and then of all the floors this boy was getting off it had to be mine! I tried to act like I knew where I was going, so I went in the opposite direction he went in. When I saw him turn the corner, I peeked around the corner in the direction he went and saw him enter into an apartment.

I looked at the apartment number on the door and, yup, he went into the apartment I was going to. "Nope, not today! Not for me!" I screamed in my head. I pushed for the elevator to come and luckily in all those few minutes the elevator was still there. I got on and, honey, when I hit the sidewalk I was off and walk/running so fast. It was just something about that one that didn't sit well with my soul.

I can say it like that now because I know, but back then, all I knew was that my stomach seemed to hit the floor. I went through a few more clients after that until I was placed with two of the warmest and loving individuals I would meet and I was home. But working in that field, you get close; "catch feelings" as the saying goes. Well, I did anyway. And there I stayed until 1995.

In spite of feeling like family and not wanting to leave them, I had to make some moves. The job was pretty much minimum wage save for a few extra dollars an hour. I needed more and I wanted back into what I called the "real world," the "business world," "the city."

I missed that. I no longer cared for smelling ammonia and bleach every day, mopping and doing laundry as a job. I did this enough at home. I lost so much time and both of my dear friends were diagnosed with a terminal disease. I didn't want to hang around and watch them leave, but I stayed as long as one possibly could. And this also included my own personal patriarch of my family, the one who helped kick start that journey of my life.

My dreams didn't look like that life to me! Hmmmph... humble beginnings! Dif*fer*ent Not the same as another or each other; unlike in nature, form, or quality. Wish I'd had someone to explain that to me back then. Explain why I was the one that sat by the wayside, on the bench, overlooked, misunderstood. Why did my voice sound so childlike?

No one took me seriously. Not even the one I needed the most. I was never told that I wouldn't be anything but I wasn't encouraged to be, either. It was just...go to school, graduate, and get a job. That was accomplishment enough.

I was told that I could be anything I wanted, do anything I wanted. I was told to reach toward the sky for it is limitless. "The world is an oyster," I had heard many say. But for whom? I wondered. Yeah, I wondered until yesterday! I had always felt like I was different. I always felt alone, by myself. I had friends, though not many. But then again, was I mistaking them for friends when they were just people I knew at that moment? Good question.

Thinking back, I used to write a lot. Poems (at least I thought they were) and short stories with a classmate in elementary school. I was horrible at drawing, so she did that. I wrote endlessly in journals or back then they were called "diaries."

I wrote about everything, and then one day it was all gone. That feeling had all but disappeared; I never sat down to think about when. So much had happened in my short forty-five years. However, due to those trials, tribulations, and some light afflictions, I now know they were building a testimony. For me and you, reader, and maybe one that has a similar situation or knows of someone else that does. Know that you are fearfully and wonderfully made in the Lord's image. Don't believe me? It's in the written Word of the Holy Bible.

Reader I believe with my whole heart that God is. And throughout this journey of life, I am to this day dif-fer-ent and unique and special and valuable and worth all that God has in stored for me. I use past tense because it's already done and waiting for me to catch up. And you should know this, too!

Through it all, you are love and cared for. For He knows the plans that He has for you... *** So many pretty women to choose from and I was favored. Favored by the attention of someone I was apprehensive about knowing. I grew up hearing about him, some of the great things he'd done for people but I wondered what he could do for me?

A struggling single parent to a teenage boy with one marriage down the drain. (Yes, his father was there; however, he was hardly ever there.) Thank God I got called for an apartment in the PJ's. It's rough out there living to pay bills, food, clothes, and the little incidentals you need daily. Just didn't seem right. I didn't grow up always seeing the happy husband and wife two-parent home. But somehow, I knew what it was supposed be.

I always felt that I was supposed to be a wife and mother with the house on the hill and white picket fence with the dog, cat, and car. And, yet, when I opened my eyes every morning this is what I didn't see. I was invited to church one day to see my coworker dance. Well, I had been away from the church for quite some time and never had seen or heard of praise dancing in church before. Needless to say, I accepted but I didn't go.

I so-called dated a few people. That is, if by standards or Webster's definition of dating is what you could call it. Then, yeah, I did that! By church standards I was in the world. And in between me doing my thing in the world, another friend and I were invited to church again by the same person. Now my curiosity had kicked in and I wanted to see this praise dancing. However, when the time came, I called my friend to see if she was going. When she said no, somehow I felt relieved but disappointed, too!

Was this normal? Could it be possible to be relieved and disappointed at the same time? Yup! Say what you want, that's what it was. It might have been a week later or longer and the invitation came again. Now I made up my mind that I was going and nothing and no one would stop me. Sunday morning came and I called my friend. "You going?" "No, Desi. I'm sorry.

I was supposed to call you last night." She asked me if I was going. "Yup, I'm going, and as a matter of fact, I'm almost ready to leave." Some friend I was. I should have called her earlier in case she was going and needed that phone call to wake her up, I thought.

Yet, I was excited, nervous. I didn't know why. I had not been to anyone's church in a while and truly didn't know what to expect, but I made it. One of the best decisions I could have ever made. It was as if I had never left! That I had never "only attended on holidays or Mother's Day because my grandma made me." This man here was speaking to me and I was on my feet. Next thing I knew, I was leaping. I can't really explain the feeling I felt, not even to this day. All I can say is, I knew something was different, something had happened.

I kind of blanked out for a minute. And when I became aware of my surroundings again, the pastor seemed to be looking right at me. I never told anyone this before, well, not like this. I had all sorts of questions running through my mind. What did it mean? Was he really looking at me? And why? One question was definitely answered; I had had an encounter with the Holy Spirit. That was the beginning of the end! For 2 Corinthians 5:17 says, "Therefore if any man be in Christ, he is a new creature: old things are passed away; behold, all things are become new"

Here this one goes again. What is it that he wants from me? I don't know. All of a sudden, it seems he's saying these little things. Okay...he's coming this way. If he says anything this time, I'm going to ask him. "Excuse me, Desiree," he says. "Yes?" "Can I have your phone number?" he asks. "Pastor says 'You only get one [date]' and I had my one already."

I don't remember his response, but whatever it was, I had to stop what I was doing. At that time, I was president of the cleaning committee at the church, and said, "What? What do you want from me?" His response was, "Hold up, why the hostility? I'm just asking if we could go out, have dinner, and talk?" I said, "Okay?

Go ask Pastor about that first then you can come to me." "Wait, wait a minute, we're both adults. Why do I have to ask Pastor anything? We can have dinner, talk, and come to an understanding if we want to go in that direction. Then we can talk to Pastor." Of course, I am paraphrasing right now; it has been too long to remember every little detail. But you get the picture, yes? It sounded okay, it made sense, but I was still not totally convinced.

A "Yeah, we'll see" is how I left it. I was in the choir and not until these small encounters had I ever had him on the brain. But when I think about it now, his steps were ordered by the Lord, because he saw a part of me that was genuine and pure. I cared about people in general, know you or not. The choir had to sing out a lot and not everyone had transportation of their own...namely me.

So I had to find a ride, but most times, I was with another sister/choir member and they had secured one, so I hopped in. A few times it was with the band's bass player. I would ask if he needed or wanted a few dollars for gas. He would decline and I'd be dropped off at my door, say goodnight, and be off. I cannot give an accurate number of how many times this happened but along the way, something happened.

Conversations would ensue whether we were alone or with a group of folks. I remember the choir had to sing at a church on Fulton Street. I was going straight from work. I took the 4 train to the Utica Avenue station and walked a few blocks over. As I was walking down the street looking for the church, I saw him first, as he was the tallest out of the bunch standing around talking. I walked up and said my hellos to everyone.

We stood there a few more minutes and then the circle started to disburse. I don't recall who it was standing there with us, but the conversation had something to do with talking about putting people on the spot. And he turned to me and said something about a kiss. All I remember now was he started to approach me and I stepped back and took off for the hills! Well, I ran toward the church and up the stairs I went.

I know if I brought this up to him today, he probably could tell me how it all went down. Needless to say, his memory is just that good. Fast forward! There was a woman from the church who had boys around the same age as mine. They started to hang around one another. We, as parents, thought it befitting to become chummy and see just where and who we both were. The more time they spent, the more time we spent. And I shared with her the little things this guy was saying and, you know, sharing the encounters.

Finally, one day I was telling another one of my stories and she couldn't bear to hear and not ask who this man I had been talking about was. Come to find out, he was the bass player at our church and a good friend of hers. She was so tickled to know and I guess at some point she started to devise a plan. And that plan is what started a nine-year relationship. Let me just tell you the beginning. One evening, she called me up and asked if I would be open to having a three-way conversation. Her, him, and ME?

I consented right away, of course, because I knew him already and so what? It was just a phone conversation. Harmless! We hung up and she called back; enter Mister. We talked for about four or five hours until we realized that Mister and I were the only ones talking. Our mutual friend had fallen asleep (so we thought and still do to this day). So we decided to hang up and call one another back.

I don't remember who called who back but we did and the

conversation has not ended!   Tell me God won't do it. Once you start refocusing your attention on HIM and taking care of His business, He will be more than honored in taking care of yours.   Speak those things which are not as though they were! Be bold and ask for what you want. Be careful, though, you're sure to get it! Enter center stage a big blessing in a small package.

MORE TO COME!

Questions for Reflection

1.   How have you embraced your "different?" Reflect on ways that you can acknowledge and nurture your own peculiarity.

_____

_____

_____

_____

_____

_____

2.   Imagine that you are a tree. What kind of fruit would you produce? What is your "hidden treasure?" What gifts are lying dormant inside you, waiting to be discovered? How have your life experiences influenced the gifts you've been given?

_____

_____

_____

_____

_____

_____

CHAPTER NINE

Monique's Prayer

Father, in the name of the only One who has secured our victory on Calvary, bore our sins and carried our sorrows; the One who was pierced and bruised so we can walk in liberty, Jesus Christ the risen One, we give thanks. We thank You because our pain can be healed, our shame eradicated, and our past woven beautifully into the fabric of our present and future. With our guilt erased, we can walk in the glorious light of Your love. It is Your love that sets us free, Your love that sustains us, lifts us up, and allows us to have life and that more abundantly.

Thank You Father for these selfless, courageous writers willing to momentarily lift the veil that covers their lives to share with us wounds healed by Your touch. Father, let Your uncontainable blessings saturate the lives of each author who has contributed to this volume. Let this be the beginning of an explosion of gifts and talents in the world of literature proclaiming Your love for us and desire to heal all of our hurting places. Restore to them one thousand fold all they have poured out to so many. Now Abba, as each and every contributor pours out, give each reader the willingness and capacity to receive their collective wisdom. Create an atmosphere of divine exchange with each reading. Grant us listening hearts, transformable minds, a willingness to desire change. Teach us how to love You, ourselves, and each other.

And Abba, for the dynamite who brought us together, Ms. Nisi: because you transformed her life, millions will be transformed. Wildly exceed her expectations, let the blessing of one thousand times more abide in her life, and most of all set her in the center of You and You be the center of all that she is … I ask these blessings in the name that is above every name, Jesus the Christ, the Risen One.

Amen.

Two Words

"If the Son therefore shall make you free, ye shall be free indeed."
John 8:36

I caught my yawn just as it was about to escape my lips. If Nia caught me with that bored look on my face during praise and worship, I'd have to endure a lecture longer than the sermon I was not looking forward to that day. I have loved the Lord for as long as I can remember.

There is not a single memory that doesn't include God in some way, shape, or form. But recently I was beginning to feel like I was in trouble, like I was slowly drowning in nothingness. A vacation from church sounded more and more appealing every time I thought about it.

The thought made me laugh out loud but I coughed to cover it up; laughing in church would certainly draw ire. "Focus, Beth. Focus on Nia's voice," I whispered to myself. Nia, an anointed worship leader, was belting out "I Surrender All." There was not a dry eye in the house. She was like the sister I almost never had, replacing the sister I lost contact with so many years ago. She knew me the longest and held all my secrets. One look and she would see the turmoil in my soul.

Closing my eyes, hands toward heaven, I silently pleaded, "God why can't I feel You? I know You're here because You're everywhere but that means nothing to me in this moment." I can do church in my sleep, but in this moment, I couldn't muster the energy to go through the motions.

"Hallelujah!" "Glory!" "Thank You Jesus!"

These phrases clanked around me so loudly I could hardly hear myself think. The air seemed filled with confusion and desperation with a sliver of sadness. Gone were the days of awe, wonder, and the greatness of our God. Forgotten was the palpable belief that "God is gonna do it" charging the air, the feeling that made you open your eyes because God felt that close.

An irritating nudge from the usher snapped me back into the present as I made room for the gentleman seeking a seat. I gave up on trying to worship and simply closed my eyes. Elder Leyan was screaming and yelling at God like He was asleep. "Who am I and why am I having these thoughts? God is great and greatly to be praised! Oh Lord, You are worthy!"

All the right words and nothing. I am going to reach out and talk with someone, I thought, but scanning the sanctuary immediately changed my mind. I would lose not only my positions but the respect I had earned. I could never regain that back. Beth, let's just get through this service with the man of God screaming and all.

I glanced over at the gentleman seated next to me, tears streaming down, his head bowed, and hands upturned in his lap. I wanted to be there, in that place with God. I wanted to place my hand in His like a child. It seemed intrusive but I desperately needed to feel something. As I closed my eyes again, I felt it.

Rising from the corner of my heart, the shadow was trying to escape from the hidden place. Hardening every inch of my heart as it sought its path to liberation and paralyzing my mind as it crept along. The shadow—that had been its name since I was thirteen years old—was usually controllable, but today I couldn't make it return to its hidden place. This thing entered my heart one terrifying afternoon twenty years ago and has never left.

It's blocked me from totally giving myself to anyone and prevented anyone from getting too close. While it fueled my driving ambition and my emotional efficiency, it was also responsible for me being on the verge of losing the only man I've ever come close to loving.

One eye slowly opened and rested on my neighbor, enviable peace had replaced his tears. Beth, how did we get here and, more importantly, how do I leave this place? Jesus, help, please help! I am going to lose him, my mind, and You, and I can't afford to. My yesterday is killing my tomorrow! I sighed. Like lead, my eye fell and the shadow began to take shape with no control over the thoughts, the memories. Angles and definition brought the shadow into sharp focus, releasing pain like I had never felt. A hand gently resting on my own began erasing the images and easing the pain.

My neighbor whispered, "God loves you more than you know in this moment." Rage, companion to the shadow, shot from my heart and set fire to my tongue but my lips would not—could not—open. I tried moving my hand but the love-filled pressure would not let me go. Rage imperceptibly gave way to a convolution of resentment, roaring from a place behind my belly button, spreading like fire and consuming everything good in my soul.

Through the oppressive darkness I heard Nia singing slowly and deliberately, accompanied by only the keyboard, "He Was There All The Time," channeling her inner Jimmy Swaggart. Nia's voice leapt to "Mercy Rewrote My Name" and "No One Ever Cared for Me Like Jesus." The words, coupled with the love flowing from the stranger's hand, seemed to be fighting the shadow and all its tentacles.

However, I'm not so sure I want to let them to go; they had become my strong tower, my strength, my fortress, and my sense of peace. Who would I be without them? How can I live my life unprotected? My heart whispered, "Shouldn't Jesus be all that the shadow is to you?"

"One would think!" I shot back.

But when I needed Him the most, He was not there! He was not there! He left me all alone to suffer! I cried out to Him and nothing! No protection! I cried myself to sleep that night! I kept myself from losing my mind! I did the right thing, I spoke up, I told adults, and they used the information against me, and He watched.

I sat in church week after week dying and no one noticed that I had changed, that I'd become withdrawn and surly. So I learned to live with pain and church in my heart. I spoke the language, lived the culture, but held God and His people at a polite distance.

The pressure on my hand was now too much. Resisting the overwhelming urge to pull my hand away, I gave up, totally let go. In an instant, the floodgates in my soul opened and everything became one. Then silence, total silence, and, from a distance, a voice screaming, "Where were you? I needed You and You were not there!"

Shrieking like an animal caught in a trap, the sound was gut wrenching. Opening my eyes to find the source, I found everyone staring at me. It took me thirty seconds to realize that the wellspring of guttural sounds was erupting from my own mouth.

TO BE CONTINUED!

Questions for Reflection

1.   Many of us have deeply painful memories living within us, trapped inside, and waiting for their release. Maybe you didn't get justice for evil in your childhood. Maybe you were abandoned or neglected. Take this space to release your rage, resentment, and regret to God. Say how you really feel. Don't hold back. Then leave it on the page. Move forward in life (through therapy and (re)building relationships with others) and with God.

_____

_____

_____

_____

_____

_____

2.   Use this space to reflect on your worship life. Be honest with yourself. How are you doing? Are you only worshipping in church, while neglecting invoking God's presence in your home? Are you acknowledging His greatness daily? Do you need to seek out resources to better understand what worship is all about? Take the time here to outline ways you can increase the frequency and quality of worship in your life.

_____

_____

_____

_____

_____

_____

CHAPTER TEN

Jonea's Prayer

Dear God,

I pray that You encourage us to turn to Your ways. I pray that our mind will stay on You. Thank You for Your hand of protection toward me and people in this world. Thank You for waking us up every morning, because if it wasn't for You, we wouldn't be alive in Your presence.

Draw us closer to You in the name of Jesus. I'm praying that You encourage those that have been negative to do positive in Your ways, God. Thank You for covering me and my family under the blood. Wash us in Your blood in the name of Jesus. We thank You for dying on the cross for our sins. I ask that whoever reads my story will be blessed and encouraged to want to know You, in Jesus' name.

Amen.

Be Yourself

"And be not conformed to this world: but be ye transformed by the renewing of your mind,
that ye may prove what is that good, and acceptable, and perfect, will of God."
Romans 12:2

My name is Jonea Thompson and I'm a thirteen-year-old girl from Freeport, New York. My hobbies are reading, writing short stories, basketball, dance, and my absolute favorite: doing people's hair. I also enjoy surfing the internet, watching television, riding my bike, and, most importantly, spending time with my friends and family. I really believe that spending time with family is important.

The reason that it's important is because I love all of them and it's a time that we all talk to each other. Oftentimes, we play family games and go on local family trips or out to eat. I really enjoy these times with them. This summer we spent a few days at the pool learning to swim and just having fun together.

I know that I will remember these times when I get a little older and that's why it's special to me.   I will write about encouragement. The reason that I chose to write on this topic is because it's what I needed in my last school year and I am sure I will need it again in the future. Last school year was very long and there were many times that I needed encouragement.

The word encouragement means "giving support of confidence and hope". Giving encouragement shows honor, hope, peace, and support.   People need encouragement when they are struggling with certain problems. They have problems in school, work, with friends, enemies, children, and even with family. I would like to share some of my obstacles and how I was able to overcome them through encouragement.

During the 2014-2015 school year, I was a fifth grade student. In the beginning of the year, my teacher and I had a good relationship. She often said kind words about me and gave me special privileges.

She would say I'm a responsible and hardworking student. She would let me check and grade other students' work and help her around the classroom. She even allowed me to use her iPad. The teacher set high goals for me and expected good grades.

From the start of the year, I listened and had good grades but then something changed. During the school year, I began to make friends with some of the students in my classroom.

They acted irresponsibly and behaved badly. They were laughing while doing work and while the teacher was teaching. They were being disrespectful by talking back to the teachers and not following directions. Some of them were acting a bit jealous because I was a hardworking student who was given privileges.

I was acting like a leader, and because of that, they didn't really like me. It made me sad, so, in my mind, I thought I had to change my ways. I pretended that their mistreatment didn't bother me on the outside, but on the inside, I felt crushed and unhappy. I was unhappy with myself because I wanted those people to like me but their actions weren't right.

I started getting smart with teachers, getting angry, and having problems with other people. I even called people that I didn't like mean names. My teacher began to notice my harmful actions and decided to have a conversation with me. She spoke to me about my actions and how I started to follow my new friends. She told me my grades were getting low, so I had to step it up.

I already knew why they didn't like me; I just wanted to fit in with them. It made me doubt myself. I felt alone and wanted to switch classes if I didn't fit in with them. I really wanted them to like me. I used to be excited getting up in the mornings for school; now I didn't want to get up because in the class I felt alone and disliked by other students in the class.

I began to go through some problems in school. I was making fake friends and misbehaving. I was being influenced by their behaviors. The devil wanted me to be like them so I prayed and asked God to help me. I asked Him to help me to do well in school and not to be like other people around me. That's when I realized that I can't be like everyone else; I have to be myself because God made me to have my own personality.

I wanted to be a leader, not a follower. I didn't want bad things to start happening. I didn't want low grades and to be known for not listening to teachers. I began to think about how I started in September. I had a good report card and my grades were very high. But in the middle of the school year, I started goofing around, making friends laugh, laughing when the teacher was teaching. The more I thought about it, I said, "This isn't the real me." I continued to pray about it.

The more I prayed, I realized that I'd stopped doing the things I was doing. The students in my class started to see the changes in me. I was really surprised when they started to compliment my decision to make better choices.

Toward the end of the school year, my grades improved and I graduated with a 6th grade diploma and six trophies. Some of my friends got few trophies and I could see the disappointment in them. I was so happy that God encouraged me to do better in school and to be a leader not a follower.

"Brothers and sisters, God had shown his mercy. So I am asking you to offer your bodies to him while you are still alive. Your bodies are a holy sacrifice that is pleasing to God. When you offer your bodies to God you are worshipping him in the right way. Don't live the way this world lives.

Let your way of thinking be completely changed. Then you will be able to test what God wants for you. And you will agree that what he wants is right. His plan is good and pleasing." To me this means that I shouldn't follow what other people in the world do. Let your mind focus on what God wants for you to achieve in life. Follow your own path—don't be a follower, be a leader. I really appreciate the love and support from God and the people that encouraged me.

Please be on the lookout for my full book!

Questions for Reflection

1.   The Bible says, "But ye are a chosen generation, a royal priesthood, an holy nation, a peculiar people; that ye should shew forth the praises of him who hath called you out of darkness into his marvellous light" (1 Peter 2:9, KJV). As one of God's chosen, how do you practice "declaring His praises" in your daily life? What do you do that sets you apart from others and gives God glory? (Hint: it doesn't have to be something big, fancy, or grand.)

_____

_____

_____

_____

_____

2.   The Bible also says, "If ye were of the world, the world would love his own: but because ye are not of the world, but I have chosen you out of the world, therefore the world hateth you." (John 15:19, KJV) Reflect on a time when it seemed as though someone (or a group of people) hated you for not being "of the world". Were you tempted to join them or seek worldly vengeance? How did you overcome that situation?

_____

_____

_____

_____

_____

_____

CHAPTER ELEVEN

Otis's Prayer

There should not be any surprise: everyone will face many trials and tribulations. But in the midst of everything that is going on in this world, nevertheless, God still has not told a lie concerning the wiles of the devil and our many trials and tribulations. I believe my life's experiences are vehicles to someone's deliverance, healing, and blessings. I pray that lives are transformed. I pray that dreams are revisited. I pray that purpose is fulfilled. I pray that all God's promises for you, dear reader, are what you receive. Our destiny is to leave a legacy!

Amen.

The Best of Both Worlds

Is this a dream, or is it real? Am I capable, or am I unqualified? Why me? These are just some of the many questions that swirl in my mind while on a mission that brings second guessing. Fear of the answers have brought doubt, paralyzing forward progress. Facing my questions gave me the assurance of God's precise timing, accuracy, and on point abilities.

I give thanks for my questions and doubts because it reveals how much God loves me by calming my spirit as His child. The moment and time is right now, so this is a real dream manifesting. All things are possible; so I can just believe, receive, and achieve.

I can do all things with Christ, automatically stamping and validating me; therefore, I am going to share a particular testimony on how God's hand of protection and grace was over my life. Before I proceed, allow me to start from the very beginning.

October 25th, 1975 is the day and year to be remembered. The hospital was Mercy Hospital, and the clock struck 4PM. The time had finally come. A strong, bubbly baby boy entered the world to Henry and Ernestine Becoat. His name is Otis Jermaine Becoat. New York is the state and Hempstead is the town where it all begins. In 1976, our apartment complex on Terrace Avenue caught on fire. The fire destroyed everything, forcing my family to move to the other side of Hempstead on Martin Luther King

Drive. "D block" was the street's nickname.

My parents raised me in the church. Church was first and foremost—and mandatory. Church was every day, and church never seemed over. My father is an elder and my mother is an evangelist. My mother was the nurturer, and she raised me up to obey God's word. She was a stickler who always stayed on my behind to stay on the straight and narrow.

My father, on the other hand, was the bread winner and military dad. He favored the scripture Joshua 24:15. It reads, "And if it seem evil unto you to serve the LORD, choose you this day whom ye will serve; whether the gods which your fathers served that were on the other side of the flood, or the gods of the Amorites, in whose land ye dwell: but as for me and my house, we will serve the LORD." There were no exceptions; every member of the Becoat's residence—my mom, my brother, and myself—had to abide by that command, even the pet.

Franklin Elementary School is where my schooling started, from kindergarten to sixth grade. Since my childhood, I was known as a class clown and a troublemaker. My mom stayed at the school because of my behavioral problems.

My first grade teacher hit me in the back of my head, which caused my tooth to hit the desk and crack. The school recommended putting me in Special Education classes due to my constant denial to listen.

My mom refused to believe that her son belonged in Special Education classes. Before I graduated from Franklin Elementary, I was placed in the talented and gifted class alongside the other kids with top honors. My parents did not want me to stay in the Hempstead School District.

The next stop was St. Agnes Elementary School, a Catholic

school. This was a culture shock to me since I was accustomed to being in public schools. I interacted mostly with kids who didn't share the same skin color, economic status, or religious beliefs.

My environment changed suddenly, but my behavior remained the same. The discipline at this school was much more severe than at my elementary school. The school called my parents and threatened to expel me if my behavior continued and did not show improvement.

Changing the clocks, running the hallways, talking in class, and switching the bad grades to good grades on my report card gave the school more than ample reason to respond in such a manner. I survived those two years without being kicked out.

Kellenberg Memorial High School was the school I attended from ninth through twelfth grades. These six years of Catholic schooling were torture to me. Living in the projects just made it worse. There was constant mocking, teasing, and laughing from the kids on the block that went to the public schools. My morning dress consisted of slacks, tie, penny loafers, and a blazer; on top of this, I waited on the bus while all the kids were looking at me and laughing. It was a horrible experience that I would not ever forget, but it was worth every minute. Kellenberg Memorial High School set the foundation for my future being bright because of their priority in making students become college ready. Upon my completion of twelfth grade at Kellenberg, I was accepted to such colleges as NYU, Wagner, and Syracuse University.

My desire was to go to Syracuse, but the cover was pulled back and revealed on different family matters that prohibited my desire from coming true. My dreams were burst like a bubble when I was made to fill out the application to Nassau Community College. I was accepted and my parents enrolled me in.

Going to Nassau Community College was worse than my high school years; all the kids teased me even more now that we all ended up at the same destination for school. They mocked me even more for wearing the uniforms for six years straight, and now not having any stylish clothes to be one of the cool guys.

I became a rebel during my college years. I felt betrayed and embarrassed. I felt that all my hard work and goals that I had accomplished were in vain, so I started on a downward spiral.

In a two-year school, I made my enrollment to Nassau Community College a journey. Many years later, I was still taking college courses there. Never once did I take my classes seriously, and I paid for it. Unbelievably, I was able to fool my parents into believing I was doing well. My enrollment sheet with my credits for my classes was deceivingly given to my parents as my transcript. My parents boasted on my false success and even threw me parties.

How I was able to be a part of helping with the women's basketball team is still a mystery to me, but I will chalk it up to God's favor in my life. Eventually, though, it all crumbled. The lies, deception, manipulation, and schemes all came to an end when my mother had a dream one night. The following morning, my mom asked me if I had anything to tell her. She said, "God woke me up!"

I knew the end was now. I finished Nassau with about twenty-two credits, including fifty-two withdrawals and a few F's. At this stage of my life, I decided to work and give school a break. Jobs were always easy for me to find but hard for me to keep. I have been working since I was sixteen years old. Between the ages of sixteen and twenty-one, I worked at the beach, banks, schools, etc.

But one year, I found a job that changed my life forever. Twenty-one and I was smelling my britches; this is an old school expression referring to thinking oneself older than what you are. The person thinks they are grown and lacks the respect to abide by rules given to them. I went against all my family teachings. I was bold in the fact that I didn't have to ask my mom or dad for permission to go anywhere.

This thought process was so far from the truth, but I lived in a fantasy world of my own.

One weekend night, I was driving my 1988 Dodge Aries station wagon. I saw a club that grabbed my attention. I walked in and my eyes opened in such awe. I was seeing something that I saw very little of: many beautiful, sexy ladies walking around making money for being topless and dancing. This was a new world to me, and I liked it. There were many problems with me being in this club.

First of all, I was not old enough to get in the club. My legal age was old enough to be in the club, but the club's age rules were twenty-five and up. Second of all (which should have been first of all), the club allowed smoking cigarettes inside of the club, and I still lived with my parents. Third of all, every Sunday was still a family principle to get up and go to church. I had to comply with that no matter what time I would come home; I still had to rise and shine every Sunday morning.

I had to think of a plan to make this all work. The light bulb was above my head; I decided to leave my coat and suit jacket in the car. This prevented the smell of smoke from sticking to my clothes. I walked back to the door and out of the shadows came a much bigger man. He asked for my I.D.; I told him that I was already in the club, and my I.D. was in the car.

The first big man, may he rest in peace, came to the door and vouched for me being in the club earlier. The two went back and forth about me not having my I.D., determining if I could go in without it; this was the most crucial moment. If I was told to go back to the car to get my I.D., I would have left and not returned until I was old enough. That would have been four years later, but they let me back in. Whew!

My Kool-Aid smile illuminated the club. The club was dark with light effects throughout. Men were drinking and smoking; there was nudity and loud music. I got my first dance ever. This seductive dancer whispered in my ear, and I let her dance all over me. She finished and asked for her money. I didn't know the rules and didn't have enough money, so she threatened to tell the biggest guy at the door. Earlier that night, I'd seen him knock out two people already for not paying the girls.

I begged and pleaded with the dancer not to say anything, and I promised to come back the next day to pay her. She gave me a chance and never told. I went home with a sigh of relief and excitement for the next night to go back. Owing her money was my pass to come back the following night.

I went back to pay, and I was remembered and never carded. I wound up talking to one of the bouncers working the girls on the stage; we bonded almost instantaneously. He asked me a question that caused me to enter into a dark world.

"Would you mind doing me a favor?"
"What is that favor?"
"Would you mind working this weekend for me?"
"What would I have to do?"
"You would just have to watch the stage."
I said yes.

That one weekend turned into ten and a half years. I went from being in the club two nights a week to being there from Monday through Saturday. I started living a club lifestyle of sin beyond imagination. My attitude changed from being nice to mean and an aggressor. People that had known me before looked at me like a stranger. Deeper, deeper, and deeper I fell into oblivion. Sin was my only option.

I was gambling, partying, sexting, fighting, smoking, and drinking. My mother worried nightly, constantly pleading for me to quit. I ignored her wishes, but she continually prayed for God to intervene. And God did intervene. My mother's prayers were answered when my pastor, Frank Anthone White, allowed me to be his adjutant. I was most unqualified, but God had a plan.

My pastor took me under his wing despite what I told him I did at my job. I left the club on Sunday mornings at 6:45AM to meet my Pastor to drive him from Freeport to Southampton. During those times, Pastor would enlighten me with words of wisdom and golden nuggets. I battled with being in the best of both worlds, but I had to choose one master.

Every scary moment that I encountered at the club, my Pastor received a call from me asking for a word of prayer. "How many warnings do you need?" is what he always asked me. I answered another one, because I knew I would be back the next day. The war between the spirit and flesh was real.

December 22nd, 2007 was the Christmas party, and I was dancing and having a good time. After being talked to a couple of times, a young man had to be thrown out of the club. The other bouncer did the duty, and I went to get some ice. The next few events changed my perspective on life forever. My boss ordered one of the customers, who was a regular, to get the ice instead of me.

I went outside to check on the other bouncer, who had been outside for way too long. He was about six-foot-six and 270 pounds. The guy thrown out was about five-foot-ten and 180 pounds soaking wet.

I felt something was wrong, and indeed it was. Suddenly, I was in a scene from the Matrix. I saw everything in slow motion even though life was still moving in real time. I saw the guy pull a huge knife out of his pocket; he went to slice the bouncer's neck. I had to make a painful decision either way: watch or grab the knife. I grabbed the knife, saving the bouncer, but I had to get thirteen stitches on my finger. That could have turned out much uglier than it did; both the bouncer and I could have been killed or badly injured. That Sunday I went to church and gave my life to the Lord.

I was thirty-three years old. I heard the words of my pastor saying that your decisions determine your destiny. I could never lie and say that I didn't enjoy my years in the club. I had a blast—so much so that I almost lost my soul to the devil's traps.

TO BE CONTINUED!

Questions for Reflection

1.   The Bible states: "But God, who is rich in mercy, for his great love wherewith he loved us, even when we were dead in sins hath quickened us together with Christ (by grace ye are saved;)" (Ephesians 2:4-5). Use this space to reflect on moments in your life when God granted you grace (good things we don't deserve to happen) and mercy (bad things we do deserve that don't happen).

_____

_____

_____

_____

_____

_____

2.   Psalm 133:1 says, "Behold, how good and how pleasant it is for brethren to dwell together in unity!" (KJV) Yet, so often we take for granted our spiritual homes and our leaders—their counsel, their fellowship, and the strength and protection we gain from worshiping and engaging in ministry together. Make a list of the ways in which your spiritual family has deposited blessings into your life and thank God for them. If you don't have a church home or a spiritual family, use this space to reflect on your spiritual needs and make it a point to begin your search for a place or people that meets your needs (if you haven't already).

_____

_____

_____

_____

_____

_____

CHAPTER TWELVE

Kareem's Prayer

Dear Almighty God, our Heavenly Father:

I come to You as humbly as I know how, sincere in heart, and with tears in my eyes. I pray for the person about to read this chapter right now. I pray that You forgive them of all their wrongdoings, for no one is perfect but You. I ask that you heal this person in every area of their life, where they have been abused, used, and deeply hurt. You, alone, healed me from all of my hurts and pains. I know beyond a doubt that You can do the same for them—with You nothing shall be impossible.

By the spirit and power that You have invested in me as one of Your servants, I cancel every assignment sent their way by Satan, to sidetrack and destroy their lives. I declare that NO WEAPON FORMED AGAINST THIS PERSON SHALL BE ABLE TO PROSPER!

May this person walk from this day forward in peace and in victory. May Your blessings and abundant love be with this person and their family. Bless this person's mind, heart, household, business endeavors, and their walk with You. Use this person to reach others for the better as only You can, Lord God.

I trust You to open up new doors of wonderful opportunities for this person. Bless them so well that they will never have to beg, steal, or borrow. Bless them to be a tremendous blessing everywhere they go.
In Jesus Christ's name, I pray. Thank You, Lord God. Thank You.

Amen.

The Devil Wanted Me Dead

"And they overcame him [Satan] by the blood of the Lamb,
and by the word of their testimony…"
Revelations 12:11

Many years ago, before I scored myself a first class ticket to the penitentiary—the BIG house—with a heavy load of time to serve for the feds, I was knee deep in what many call the "game," but what I refer to as "that thug life!"

At twelve years old, I put that first burner in my hand. I was gonna kill two guys for jumping on me because one of them, with whom I had had a fist fight, couldn't get the best of me.

I never did catch up with those two guys while in the heat of my madness.

At fifteen years old, I put that burner in my hand again; this time, to stick up some foreign drug dealers. I didn't rob these guys because I was a hardcore thug at that time in my life; I did it because I had a child on the way that I had to take care of. I was broke and without a job; when an old-head hustler I often kicked it with in my neighborhood presented the opportunity for me to come up on that fast cash the thug way, I jumped at the chance.

When all was said and done, nineteen eggs of raw and twenty-seven g's was my reward.

I was at that point what many would call "that nig" in my hood. I had the money, the medicine (crack), and a gang of young neighborhood hoodlums who would back whatever shot I called. In the streets, we call that having "the muscle."

Before I knew it, at age sixteen, I had ignorantly dropped out of school to pursue hustling and the thug life full-time.

My mother, who raised my siblings and me alone, naturally and rightly disapproved of my decision to be involved in underworld activity. Being the thug that I had become, though, I was hardheaded, bent on doing what I wanted to do. Like any wise mother in my mom's situation, she continued loving me but had enough sense to recognize that it was time to put me in God's hands.

I can remember talking on the phone outside of my mother's apartment one day, when a car pulled up in front of me, just a few feet away. The driver stopped the car but left the engine running. While in deep conversation on the phone, I paid little attention to this car…

…that is, until I suddenly saw a gun pointing directly at my chest.

BAM! BAM! BAM!

Three shots were fired before I dropped the phone and went down. The car burned rubber.

This is my last day on earth, I thought, waiting to feel the burning sensation of the three bullets fired at my chest. But to my surprise, not one bullet touched me. Thank God for praying mothers!

You would think that surviving that murder attempt on my life would have moved me to take a different course, but you know what? I continued, thugging harder.

Next thing I knew, at seventeen, I was arrested on a laundry list of overt acts, including murder and narcotics violations. When all was said and done, I was on my way to the Big House, with forty-five years to serve in a system that had long abolished parole. That meant I would have to do 85% of my sentence before being released.

When I got to prison with all that time to serve, I seriously didn't know if I would make it or not. The Big House wasn't a "kitty camp"; it was where the government sent the most hardened criminals: mob bosses, gang chiefs, murderers, and big drug dealers. It's a place where nearly everyone carries a knife, or what is commonly known in the joint as a shank.

My homie gave me a shank shortly after I arrived, for my protection. At the same time, he sat me down and dropped it on me about the do's and don'ts of prison life. "Lil' homie, mind your business in this place. Don't do drugs, don't gamble, and don't mess with gumps (gays). And, lil' homie, just like the streets, don't let no one in here play you for a sucka."

He told me I should think about finishing school and that I should study my legal case for possible loopholes, so that I could get out sooner.

It took me some time to get my head together to do anything positive and constructive, because that street life spirit was still heavily on, and in, me.

But as I began taking small steps toward doing better and getting my act together, in no time I had gotten my GED and had taken countless education and vocational courses, including drug use prevention, anger management, parenting, and law. The more I took advantage of the time I had to serve, the less attention the thug in me received.

Anything that you don't give attention to becomes dead.

After years of putting into practice doing positive things, I discovered a gift that I had no idea I had—the gift of writing. As long as I was out there in them streets thuggin', I didn't have the chance to discover this gift.

In my nineteenth year here in prison, I received what I would call a long-awaited blessing from God. A lawyer that had been assigned to my case due to a recent change in crack cocaine laws informed me that my sentence had been reduced by ten years!

I got on my knees and thanked God for that blessing, for all good things come from Him.

Now, don't get me wrong, I'm not a "religious" guy, talking this God stuff because I'm in the joint with nothing else to do. No, that's not me; I don't believe in being a phony. There are enough of them in this world and in prison. I believe in spirituality: man tapping into his true godly nature, man connecting and cooperating with the God within, if you will. I do this through the teachings of Jesus, as is recorded in the Holy Scriptures.

Over the many years that I have been incarcerated, though, God, through His spirit, has taught me a laundry list of important things for my growth and development as a man. One of the greatest things I have learned is that no matter how hard ones falls from their upright, godly nature; that person can get back up again. No one is perfect or flawless, but you don't have to use the excuse of being imperfect to wallow in the mud of your shortcomings if you don't want to, either.

Moreover, I have learned that the streets don't make men nor do they make ladies; the streets make pimps, whores, thugs, killers, thieves, liars, and cheaters. The Lord God alone makes men and women. Sometimes He has to do so using places like prison, where one can focus and be free from the distractions of the hustle and bustle of that street life.

Some of God's greatest servants and prophets had to experience prison or some other place of isolation. It is there that one receives a revelation from God. John, author of Revelations, was on a lonely island, isolated from the wicked world of his day, when God began appearing to him, instructing him to pen what would befall the human race in the last days.

The prophet Muhammad was in a cave fasting when the angel Gabriel began appearing to him with instruction from God for him to write what would later become known as the Holy Koran.

I'm not comparing myself to either of those humble servants of God; I'm just a thug-turned-thinker by God's permission and grace. However, like those servants, my incarceration has served as a place for healing and hearing from God, so that I would become aware of my true calling in this life.

I couldn't see my purpose at first because that street life had me blind. But now, all praises due to God, I can see.

LOOK OUT FOR THE FULL BOOK!

Questions for Reflection

1.   Worldly prison is a lonely, scary place, but Biblically, prison/captivity is also a place of growth, redemption, and deliverance (Joseph, Peter, Paul). What is your prison? What is the thing (or things) that have you bound? Briefly reflect on them here, then meditate on them daily. (Tip: their opposites can go on your vision board!) Ask God to free you from your chains. Speak those things that be not as though they were!

_____

_____

_____

_____

_____

2.   "Anything that you don't give attention to becomes dead." Think about the people, relationships, places, and things in your life that no longer need your attention. (Hint: this may take more than one writing session—ask God for guidance!) List them here then forget about them. This is their graveyard!

_____

_____

_____

_____

_____

_____

My Message Is In My Mess

CHAPTER THIRTEEN

Felisia's Prayer

Heavenly Father, I pray that those who read these words and this prayer shall be changed by the power that destroys yokes and carries the burden away. Father, I pray that the word that is alive in us shall never cause us to thirst after this water has been given to us. In Jesus' name and it is so.

Amen.

Hurt

"But whosoever drinketh of the water that I shall give him shall never thirst; but the water that I shall give him shall be in him a well of water springing up into everlasting life."
John 4:14

I am like the woman at the well, drawing, drawing, pulling water into my thirsty soul. My soul is dry and my bones are wanting, like life for life, for the refreshing of the rain; the water that gives me life!

I compare my life to the woman at the well, as wanting. I was the child that God had great plans for, even though I did not know it at the time. There was an unseen world that knew all about it. Why else would I suffer such spiritual attacks at such a young age? My sleep was their way of seeing to it that I would carry a burden with me for years to come: fear. But why did He not save me from the horrors and terror of nightmares? God knew. He knew what was in my future.

Fast forward to my childhood. Oh how I began to long for my dad! Although my dad was not in our lives, I knew beyond a shadow of a doubt that he loved me. I felt his love as a child.
We lived in a middle class neighborhood in Flushing, Queens that was ethnically integrated. I was a tomboy; I wanted to, and I did, play rough. The neighborhood kids would gather together at our house and we'd partner up and strategize our ball games, build go-carts, have bicycle races, build race ramps, have arguments and make up. Then there were the bullies in the 'hood who hated our brown skin. They'd pitch fights by throwing rocks and calling us niggers. "Go back to Africa you black niggers!" I was pumped and never ran; that was my home.

My mom would dispel it, saying, "You are somebody. You have just as much right to be here as they do. You are somebody." At thirteen, I read the entire book of Revelation. I didn't understand it, but I believed. We didn't have a regular place of worship, so we often visited places from time to time. My maternal grandparents were Baptist, but Big Ma converted to a Jehovah's Witness, and summer visits to the Hall were sure. Our mom loved us; I knew she did, because she supplied for us, protected us, and defended us. She would fight for us. She was the lioness of all lionesses. Mom read the Bible and she'd school us on some of its teachings.

By seventeen, I had not yet known what it is to be a girlfriend, but I knew I didn't want to have sex. My friends were dating and engaging in sexual intercourse. I was curious about it, though. Images were everywhere and teens were hooking up. I was the laughing stock of my friends; I wanted to wait for marriage before having sex and children.

The plan: I would be married after college, have four children—two girls and two boys—be a registered nurse practitioner specializing in pediatric care, and dancing would be my art. They laughed me to scorn! We just didn't think alike concerning relationships.

L.D. appeared out of nowhere on a small moped, safely donned in a helmet and big eyeglasses. He was nice and respectful toward me at all times. But R.S. appeared with a catcall and he pushed until he got my attention and my number. Out of "kindness" I accepted his number. I played right into his hand, got roped in, played, and discarded rather quickly. He left his fingerprint in my soul and I was hurt.

You didn't give me time to love or to feel anything about you! You didn't allow me the option to say yes or no. You just lured, lied, deceived, used, and discarded. I hate you! I hate you! I love you! I love you! Don't do this to me!

I was an emotional wreck. That unpleasant encounter left me feeling oddly "grown up," "experienced," and sadly wishing for his presence. I was none of those things. Something was on me and I didn't know how to release it.

I was now a high school grad and decisions had to be made. I chose the armed forces for two reasons over the local college: one, to relieve the burden of paying for college from Mom and two, to travel to another country to work as a nurse. I successfully passed the entrance exams, including the physical, but an obstacle had arisen in the finalization of my entry and Mom wasn't happy nor was she cooperative. She insisted that I attend business school. I had no desire to do so, but I had to make a decision. How was I going to pursue my dream? I opted out and submitted to her request.

While window browsing, and mesmerized by the displays, E.P. showed up beside me. He talked and the "nice me" foolishly stood and listened. After a lengthy conversation of nothingness, and upon his begging for my number, I surrendered. Ugh! Why didn't I give him a wrong digit?

I looked forward to going to school. It was exciting and I was moving forward. Then E.P.'s phone call came. I wasn't ready for this. I was only eighteen years old. What did I know? I wanted to go to college. I needed to be in class where I belonged but it would escalate to the sorrowful plea to come.

I was naive, and I tried not to read into everything or question matters. I was timid and slow to ask questions. I further assumed that he knew what he was doing, as he was older and "in control." It was not until the damage had been done that my perception shifted. I assumed that the one who I allowed to lead me into the mess was also the one who'd be able to get me out, only to find that he had no answers. I entrusted my innocence to the hands of the hurt. Guess what happens? I hurt.

One month later, I was looking for my period, to the date I so carefully followed. Maybe I calculated it wrong. My heart skipped beats. Fear and guilt filled me. I hated these feelings. I was ashamed in the company of my friends who had previously aborted their pregnancies and had gone on with their lives. The thought to abort was there, but the fear was greater. My friends insisted that it would be best for me and the baby. Anxiety and fear were widespread. I resorted to hiding my secret from my family.

I continued to work and attend school, but that would cease due to the development of a menacing, insatiable, and prickling annoyance of the skin encompassing the vestibule of the vagina. I have never known this itch in my entire life. I couldn't bear it! I described the symptoms to the doctor and he examined me, and returned with a diagnosis. I was prescribed a medication and released. There was no educating me about STD's. Find out and treat. I educated myself about sexually transmitted diseases. I was embarrassed, hurt, and felt dirty. I had never known the world of STD's, and there I was in the midst. When I shared this with E.P., he denied having any responsibility. "Lie! You are the only person I have been with!" I declared with a broken heart. Oh, and yes I was pregnant. Broken and brokenhearted I didn't even see my dreams slowly slipping away. There was no one there to catch me or to encourage me. I felt like I was failing and falling.

We were gathered in my bedroom with my mom. It was beautiful. I loved having my family in one room talking, laughing, and teasing each other. We had moments in our family where it seemed like nothing else mattered, as long as we had each other. I hid under my baggy pink flannel pajamas as we chatted among each other. Yet, she did not know that her daughter was already pregnant. Soon I would submit to the authority of my mother and inform her of my secret. Time stood still. "I'm pregnant." Her expression was predictable and there was silence, then the question: "Who is the father and what are y'all going to do because you can't stay here. I have these other children that I am raising."

Then came the day that Mom would inform "E" that the baby and I are now his responsibility and he can pick me up and take me to his house. That was the end of that. No more family for me. I had disappointed her and, with pain, fear, and rejection I surrendered to her wish and regretted the day E and I met. I had to leave my family, who I loved, and pretend that I understood it all when I didn't.

Was this going to be my new life? Living with him in his brother and girlfriend's flat in the Bronx? I longed for my family but I had no choice but to settle in. I sobbed so hard with my face in the pillow that my chest ached and I held my chest to resist death by tears. When E showed up, I was glad because he was all that I had now. I trusted him to get us out of there before the baby came. He talked a good game, but no plan. There was too much that I did not know. I lacked good judgement because I lacked understanding and wisdom. I thought about college again, work, and being with my family. I was frustrated and annoyed at this so-called new life. I feared not having anything to care for this baby and I hated that he wasn't doing enough. I didn't have the fortitude to fight any of this stuff, and I needed to keep moving.

E and his brother's girlfriend were always at odds with each other; I thought that she didn't like me. Her weapon was food. Since he did not supply it for me, I could not eat her food. I didn't know what to think after he had told me what she'd said. Days came and went and I had minimum meals supplied by E. Sometimes no food at all, so I drank water and stole a slice of bread when no one was home. I woke up one morning having such hunger pangs that I thought I was going to die. I prepared a glass of sugar and water and a slice of bread, and hoped it would not be missed. I had no prenatal care for 8 months, no nutrition, no money, no health insurance, no home of my own, no support, no one checking on me, no peace, no love, no joy...empty. I was an empty shell. Feeling some relief, I made my way back to the bedroom to lay down and wept until I slept.

E's brother's girlfriend prepared a large pot of pigs' feet for herself and her friend; she invited me to eat with them. The smell filled the house and I deeply inhaled the aroma of sweet spices and marinades. This may never happen again, I thought, so I joined them and soon returned to my room. With great satisfaction, I slept without hunger pangs for almost the first time since living there.

E announced his plan for us to move out of state, and to live with his parents and two brothers. Nearing the time of my delivery, I was still without prenatal care. His family was making plans to help us by helping me through the process to receive social benefits. They were very accepting of me and, even though I was further away from my family, progress was being made in my life. I was officially a part of the welfare system that assists the poor and needy like me so that I could step up while being supported. To this day I am grateful for his family's support and the love that they showed me and our daughter. He enjoyed the life of a fatherless man. I couldn't bear it anymore.

His way of life was not my way of life. Prior to leaving New York, he said, "There's a lot that you don't know about me and

I didn't want to tell you, but I been doing drugs. It ain't just weed; I been using heroin." He showed me his arms. I thought for a minute and said, "Why don't you just stop?" He said it wasn't easy and that the help he had received was useless. I couldn't understand how help didn't help or how a person couldn't stop. I learned later in life about addictions and how they develop into strongholds that function to degenerate a mind into thinking wrongly about oneself; behavior is the evidence of that thinking.

We didn't love ourselves. I saw too many faults in my life and every time things went wrong I would curse myself with the wrong words.

His habits and the demons that were introduced into his life were not going to be my demons or our children's. I was now painfully aware that the man who had fathered my children was addicted to heroin, cocaine, and weed. When around me he was functional and well groomed. I made the decision to leave him. I cried through it, ached through it, prayed through it, visited churches through it, until the day came that I could not bleat or squall over this issue anymore.

My mind was my worst enemy, tricking me into believing that God loves everyone else except me, and that I was being punished. I still read the Bible and prayed but I was not convinced of His love even though I was saved at age sixteen. Psalm 56:8 says, "Thou tellest my wanderings: put thou my tears into thy bottle: are they not in thy book?" This scripture reminded me that God knows my thoughts and my pain. They are retrievable and memorable to Him and they will come again in joy and peace.

I could not hold onto the Word in the days of my trials but I still prayed. My heart ached even though it was over. I knew he loved his children. He was gentle toward them and he always boasted of them. The self-hatred and afflictions that tormented him were too much and he had nothing of the Lord that he would accept to be free. The spirit world is as real as the natural one you see, live in, and move in every day. Psalm 54:4 reads, "Behold, God is mine helper: the Lord is with them that uphold my soul."

I sought out answers in tarot cards, palm reading, fortune cookies, horoscope and astrology, hypnosis, and fortune telling—all in the name of finding something other than the word of God. Nothing helped me feel better. I hid myself from the Lord, thinking there was something else. I didn't know how to love and I didn't know that I was loved. Scriptures would visit my mind and I'd remember something that gave me hope. I wrote: "God is strength and God is power." I hung it up to remind me each day of God's strength.

I am fearfully and wonderfully made, God's workmanship, peculiar, and of a royal priesthood, a believer, seated in high spiritual places with Jesus, and a kingdom's child.

Years went by and I experienced more tears and more hurt, but I moved into a new direction of hope. Hope gave me a hunger for the true and living God. I began to see His passion to love me and my children. He opened my heart to possibilities. When I started caring about me and loving me, and forgiving me (which He had already done), then I began to experience sensing His love for me and for my children. I could see the Word. One of my favorite scriptures is Psalm 23: "The Lord is my shepherd..." I learned that entire scripture when I was thirteen, and now I have had to learn to allow the Shepherd to lead. May the Lord God who is in front of us be your Shepherd, and may your life be filled richly with the love of Jesus Christ.

God bless you.

———

Questions for Reflection

1.   Sometimes in life we find ourselves so fearful or downtrodden that we have little to no confidence in ourselves or the decisions that we make. Like my experiences being approached by men, we give in to that fear, sometimes doing things that we otherwise would not. Society can particularly leave women vulnerable to not believing in ourselves and showing it. What are some ways that you can build up your self-confidence? For men, what are some ways you can support the women in your life in their search for self-confidence? How can all people assert their own Godly courage? Research and reflect on scriptures and Biblical stories that show how we can have Godly courage to advocate for ourselves and stand up for our values and needs. Reflect on your own experiences.

_____

_____

_____

_____

_____

2.   The Bible often warns us against false idols, prophets, and gods. Reflect on times when you have looked to every other source for strength, answers, or a solution (a person or group, an object, etc.). How did things turn out? How can you ensure that you always "seek ye first" the ways and guidance of Christ? Use this space to reflect on those experiences and to thank God for not abandoning you in your time of doubt.

_____

_____

_____

_____

_____

WORDS OF ENCOURAGEMENT

"I was once a little girl with a dream; I became a woman with a vision."

Although my life has been complicated and painful, my pain has become my greatest motivator. It has taken my darkest hours for me to be able to see my brightest light.

Despite the things I've been through and put others through, I truly believed that I was a compassionate person, until God transformed me into the new Nisi. It was then that I began to truly love God and, as a result, my compassion for others became real. It was in my heart for sure this time. When I was the old Nisi, it wasn't a Godly compassion; if it had been, I wouldn't have been able to do and say the things that I did.

The Bible states that we've all sinned and come short of the glory of God, but no matter where you've been, what you've done, or where you are in your life today, you, too, deserve compassion and forgiveness. God is a forgiving God; He is love, and love is for everyone.

Now, as the new Nisi, I am in the business of compassion. My desire is to inspire a sense of hope in generations of the broken, to remind the lost that through healing, faith, forgiveness, and love, it is never too late to discover your purpose. I should know; I'm a living witness. And it's through my own testimony that I can proclaim that although hurt people hurt people, healed people heal people, too.

So now I turn to ask you: What is your pit? What in your life is causing you to wallow in a state of lifelessness? King David spoke of feeling as though he were in a pit, calling out to the Lord to rescue him and set his feet on solid ground.

The stories you have read are the testimonies of people from all walks of life, with many different kinds of pits. For some, they stepped into theirs unknowingly, while others willingly went in, not knowing just how deep and dark it would be. But we all have one!

Jesus is the only one who can reach deep down into our pits and lift us out of our darkness and into His glorious light because those who meet Christ change. But if you don't stretch out your arms to meet Him, He can't save you. You've got to be ready.

Are you ready to escape your pit?

AUTHOR BIOS

Denise Newsome, Project Director

Cheryl Denise Newsome is an author, playwright, producer, and director. In 2009, she independently published her first novel, Misty's Blood, which received amazing praise, leading her to adapt the book into a stage play which she produced in 2013. The sold-out show ran off-Broadway for three nights. Denise went on to write and produce another stage play, "The Birth", which premiered in June of 2016 in Hempstead, New York. Denise hails from, and currently resides in, Long Island, New York and is an active member of The Cathedral at Miracle. She is a member of the media ministry and enjoys long drives, bowling, going to the beach, and, of course, writing.

If you would like to contact or work with this author, playwright, producer, director, and motivational speaker, or reach any of the other contributing writers, please email Denise Newsome at **newsome_denise@yahoo.com**.

Kelly Exum

Kelly N. Exum is a single mother of five children and has been store manager for the same company for twelve years. She was born and raised in Freeport, New York and lived there until she moved to Fremont, North Carolina at the age of thirteen. She moved back to New York at eighteen. Ms. Exum received her New York State Cosmetology License in 1999. She began working in salons right after receiving her license. She began work with her current employer in 2001 part-time. By 2003, Ms. Exum was store manager. She is currently working on her book, titled My Life/My Testimony. She also has plans to start her own non-profit organization, The Kelly N. Exum Foundation, to help people that are suffering from gynecological cancers. She knows the struggle one faces all too well as a cancer survivor.

Sonia Spence

Sonia Spence received Christ into her life at the age of ten. She went on to participate actively in the church; at first becoming the Sunday school secretary as a teenager, then a Sunday school teacher for many years. A position opened up for the church reporter, then Youth President. She enjoyed working with youth, and made numerous changes in the ministry. Sonia enjoys talking to people and sharing her faith everywhere she goes. She is a motivator and an inspirational person. She is a widow and has one son and one grandson.

Zavier Bell

In the beginning of 1988, Zavier Bell was brought into this world. From a young age, he witnessed so much turmoil growing up in Hollis, New York. He was far too young to grasp the cause of such suffering. Through his revolutionary spirit, he knew that he had a divine responsibility— to liberate minds living in bondage. He developed a strong affinity for English and literature and began writing intensely. He is currently working on his first project, The Sixtieth Parts of a Great Hour.

Bevelyn Exume Monroe

Bevelyn was born in North Carolina and raised in Freeport, New York. Bevelyn is a retail associate in her secular job. She is an active member of The Cathedral at Miracle in Hempstead, New York. She serves as an assistant Sunday school teacher, an usher, and as a member of the Fine Arts Ministry. Her heart's desire is to see the body of Christ live up to the commands that Jesus gave, thereby drawing the unbeliever. She has two adult children: a son married with two kids; her daughter is a freelance writer, screenwriter, and activist. Ms. Monroe's hobbies include reading, floral arranging, and jewelry making. She's willing to try anything crafty and loves plants. And yes, she still likes puzzles.

Kavon Clayborn

Kavon Clayborn is the youngest of four children from the union of Charles and Anita Clayborn. Kavon has two brothers and one sister. He was born in Long Island, New York; however, he currently resides in Georgia. Personal fitness and health are extremely important to Kavon as a cancer survivor. He now enjoys sharing his passion of healthy living with others. One of his life's goals is to become a Certified Personal Trainer. Kavon would love to empower others to realize the importance of eating healthy and exercising, in order to maximize the gift that God has bestowed upon all (the gift of life).

Tonya Bradshaw

Tonya Jackson-Bradshaw hails from Freeport, New York. She attended Freeport High school, but the trials and tribulations of life lead her to drop out before graduating. In the time since, she has raised three daughters: Iesha, born in 1989; Ityra, born in 1995; and Ivanna, born in 2002. Determined to make a better life for herself, she got her G.E.D. and an Associate's degree in massage therapy, both at forty years old. She also has a degree in cosmetology. Her long term goal is to start a non-profit women's organization that focuses on domestic violence. She grew up with two sisters, Natasha Jackson and Tia Moore, and one brother, James Stevens. She enjoys serving God, doing hair, and enjoying life and her family.

Minister Desiree Richards-Johnson

Desiree Patricia Richards is a Brooklynite—born and raised—wife, and mother of two. She is a graduate of William H. Maxwell High School and holds an A.S. in Human Services from the Borough of Manhattan Community College. She currently works for DHS in New York City. Desiree is an aspiring minister, a 4Twelve Youth & Young Adult Ministry leader, Sunday School Teacher, and member of several auxiliaries within The Cathedral at Miracle, located in Long Island, New York. This is just the first installment of Hidden Treasures: The Unveiling. Desiree is standing on the promises of God for her future success.

Monique Walker

Monique Walker is pursuing a career as a life coach. Her passion is helping others to discover their purpose and embrace life. She loves Jesus, enjoys reading, and is currently working on a guide to an effectual fervent prayer life.

Jonea Thompson

Jonea Thompson was born in East Meadow, New York. She is the oldest daughter born to John Thompson and Kirra Jackson. This fall she'll be a 7th grader. Throughout her school years she has received several awards for academic achievement and behavior. In her free time, she enjoys playing basketball and running track; she also loves to do hair. One of her goals is to own several salons and create a line of hair products. She attends Miracle Christian Center under the leadership of Bishop David B. Gates, where her Christian faith has grown.

She is thankful for her strong faith in Christ taught by her Uncle Christopher and Aunt Lakisha Buckley. Jonea believes that with faith and prayer all things are possible. Jonea is a natural born leader whose ambition and drive has set her apart from her peers. When she is not doing hair or reading a book, she enjoying time with her family and friends.

Otis J. Becoat

Otis Jermaine Becoat has a Bachelor's in Business Marketing. He graduated Magna Cum Laude from Briarcliffe College. Otis is an actor, motivational speaker, and poet. He has participated in many events reciting original poetry and has recorded rap songs. Otis has hosted Black and White affairs, comedy shows, and birthday parties. He has acted in plays such as: For Better or for Worse (Racquel Marie Jones, villainous friend) A Cry for Help (Cheri McClurkin, oldest son) Misty's Blood (Denise Newsome, Off-Broadway, drug boss) Beneath The Layers (Travis Wright, undercover boss) Life Has Just Begun (Antenia Simmons, high schooler) Restoration (Antenia Simmons, Pastor) Pandora's Box (Natasha Carter, husband) The Birth (Denise Newsome, leading role)

In his spare time, he loves singing, working out, playing ball, and making people laugh. Most importantly, Otis Jermaine Becoat loves to inspire people. Our destiny is to leave a legacy.

Kareem Tomblin

Kareem Tomblin grew up in Charlotte, North Carolina, where he began hustling drugs at a young age after discovering he had a child on the way. Before he knew it, hustling was his full-time job. It lead him to prison where, after getting himself together, he became an author and novelist. One of his latest novellas is titled, My Girl Special. He is also the author of Death, No Exceptions! published in 2008 and Father Forgive Me. Many say that he is an author to watch! Kareem just wants to reach as many youth as he can with his chief message. That being said, if Christ can change a street thug like him, He can change you! He is currently awaiting his release from prison and for God to bless him with his Queen—a woman of God.

Felisia Lamb

Felisia Lamb has been an emergency room technician for fourteen years. She received an Associate's degree in Liberal Arts. She also received her certificate from MCBI in 2005 in Evangelistic Studies. Felisia is a Christian by faith and by experience she has learned what it means to "wait on the Lord and be of good courage." She has further learned to believe every word that proceeds out of the mouth of God. She learned to love intentionally and with passion after learning how deeply He loves her. She has a heart for broken women of any age with a yearning desire to see them overcome adversities and challenges they are facing in their lives so that they can move on to do great things. She has been a member of The Cathedral at Miracle, located in Hempstead, New York, since 2000. Felisia participates in the Outreach Program (street witnessing).

She dramatizes historical reenactments, both biblical and non-biblical events through the Fine Arts Ministry. Felisia teaches Sunday school Bible classes to enthusiastic adolescent students. She is a volunteer in her community at the AAA Pregnancy Options Center in Hempstead. She loves to inspire others to follow their dreams and to use their creativity to serve others. She is currently aspiring to continue and finish both nursing and ministry school and is currently working on her first book of inspirations, Dawning, which is taken from her own journals over the years.

EDUCATIONAL & SELF-HELP RESOURCES

BOOKS

Grief: Why Me? Why Not Me? A Journey of Self-Discovery (2015)
By Dr. Kiana Battle, Ph.D., LMSW and Pastor Keith Battle
Real Girls: Reflections (2011) Dr. Kiana Battle (Clayborn) & Jessica Traylor
Real Girls: Shifting Perceptions on Identity, Relationships, and the Media (2010) Dr. Kiana Battle (Clayborn) & Jessica Traylor
For information on how to purchase these books or for speaking engagements, please log on to realgirls.us or e-mail: kbattle1.kb@gmail.com.

ORGANIZATIONS & ONLINE RESOURCES

Business

National Federation for Independent Business (NFIB) – NFIB is the leading advocate for small business owners, representing 325,000 small businesses in all 50 states and Washington, D.C. It is dedicated to leveling the playing field with Big Business, Big Government, and Big Labor in every key area – taxes, healthcare, regulations, and more. Our mission is to defend the right of small business owners to run their businesses without undue government interference and to advance public policies that promote their success. We are the only major business organization whose policies and positions are established by the members directly, not by executive staff or a board of directors. That's what makes us credible, widely respected, and effective.
Website: http://www.nfib.com/business-resources/

Small Business Administration (SBA) – Established via the Small Business Act of 1953, the U.S. Small Business Administration has

delivered millions of loans, loan guarantees, contracts, counseling sessions and other forms of assistance to small businesses.
Website: https://www.sba.gov/

Cancer Organizations

American Cancer Society – For over 100 years, the American Cancer Society (ACS) has worked relentlessly to save lives and create a world with less cancer. Together with millions of our supporters worldwide, we help people stay well and get well, find cures, and fight back against cancer.
Website: http://www.cancer.org/index

National Breast Cancer Foundation – Founded in 1991, The National Breast Cancer Foundation's mission is to help women now by providing help and inspiring hope to those affected by breast cancer through early detection, education and support services.
Website: http://www.nationalbreastcancer.org/

Disability

Disability Resources, Inc. – Disability Resources, Inc. is a nonprofit 501(c)(3) organization established to promote and improve awareness, availability and accessibility of information that can help people with disabilities live, learn, love, work and play independently. We disseminate information about books, pamphlets, magazines, newsletters, videos, databases, government agencies, nonprofit organizations, telephone hotlines and on-line services that provide free, inexpensive or hard-to-find information to help people with disabilities live independently.
Website: http://www.disabilityresources.org/DRMabout.html

Domestic & Sexual Violence, Incest

NCADV (National Coalition Against Domestic Violence) - NCADV is the voice of victims and survivors. We are the catalyst for changing society to have zero tolerance for domestic violence. We do this by affecting public policy, increasing understanding of the impact of domestic violence, and providing programs and education that drive that change.

Websites: (About NCADV) http://www.ncadv.org/about-us/mission
(External resources) http://www.ncadv.org/need-help/resources

NDVH (National Domestic Violence Hotline) – Taking its first call
on February 21st, 1996, today The Hotline is still the only 24/7
center in the nation that has access to service providers and shelters
across the U.S. Don't be afraid to reach out for help!
Website: http://www.thehotline.org/

RAINN (Rape, Abuse & Incest National Network) – RAINN is the
nation's largest anti-sexual violence organization. Founded in 1994,
its programs aim to prevent sexual violence, help victims, and ensure
that perpetrators are brought to justice.
Website: https://www.rainn.org/about-rainn

Gang & Community Violence

Students Against Violence Everywhere (SAVE) – SAVE is a unique
and powerful approach to youth safety because it recognizes the role
that young people can take in making schools and communities
safer. Because SAVE chapters are established and operated by
students, the opportunity to spread the message of nonviolence to
young people and their communities is enhanced when SAVE
chapters exist. Focusing on crime prevention, conflict management
and service projects, SAVE students are providing positive peer
influences in violence prevention efforts.
Website: http://nationalsave.org/chapter-tools/resources/

Leadership Building

The Leadership Challenge - The Five Practices of Exemplary
Leadership® has proven its effectiveness in cultivating and
liberating the leadership potential in anyone – at any level, in any
organization – who chooses to accept the challenge to lead.
Website: http://www.leadershipchallenge.com/about-section-our-
approach.aspx

The Leadership Toolbox – Studying organizational development,
team building and communication develops skills that make better,
more efficient teams. The Leadership Toolbox hopes to be able to

offer all the different components that mark good leadership.
Website: http://www.leadership-toolbox.com/

Prisoner and Ex-con Advocacy
The Innocence Project - The Innocence Project, founded in 1992 by
Barry Scheck and Peter Neufeld, is a national litigation and public
policy organization dedicated to exonerating wrongfully convicted
individuals through DNA testing and reforming the criminal justice
system to prevent future injustice.
Website: http://www.innocenceproject.org/about/

The National Prison Project – A project of the American Civil
Liberties Union (ACLU), The National Prison Project is dedicated to
ensuring that our nation's prisons, jails, and detention centers
comply with the Constitution, domestic law, and human rights
principles.
Website: https://www.aclu.org/issues/prisoners-rights

Prison Activist Resource Center (PARC) – PARC is a prison
abolitionist group committed to exposing and challenging all forms
of institutionalized racism, sexism, ableism, heterosexism, and
classism, specifically within the Prison Industrial Complex (PIC).
PARC believes in building strategies and tactics that build safety in
our communities without reliance on the police or the PIC. We
produce a directory that is free to prisoners upon request, and seek to
work in solidarity with prisoners, ex-prisoners, their friends and
families. We also work with teachers and activists on many prison
issues.
Website: https://www.prisonactivist.org/about

Suicide Prevention & Mental Health
National Alliance on Mental Illness (NAMI) – NAMI, the National
Alliance on Mental Illness, is the nation's largest grassroots mental
health organization dedicated to building better lives for the millions
of Americans affected by mental illness.
Websites: (Find Support) http://www.nami.org/Find-Support.aspx
(Find your local NAMI chapter) http://www.nami.org/Find-Your-

Local-NAMI

National Suicide Prevention Lifeline – The National Suicide Prevention Lifeline provides free and confidential emotional support to people in suicidal crisis or emotional distress 24 hours a day, 7 days a week. Since its inception, the Lifeline has engaged in a variety of initiatives to improve crisis services and advance suicide prevention.
Website: http://www.suicidepreventionlifeline.org/

Psychology Today – We have gathered a group of renowned psychologists, academics, psychiatrists, and writers to contribute their thoughts and ideas on what makes us tick. We're a live stream of what's happening in 'psychology today.' Our Therapy Directory provides a comprehensive directory of therapists, psychiatrists, and treatment facilities near you. It allows you to filter for professionals who accept your insurance, those who are aligned with your spiritual beliefs, and those who meet your health needs (e.g. eating disorders, relationship issues, coping skills, grief, etc.).
Website: https://therapists.psychologytoday.com/rms/

www.ingramcontent.com/pod-product-compliance
Lightning Source LLC
Chambersburg PA
CBHW060124260626
47160CB00005B/2007